Dear Alexis

What can I...

I'm really

to miss you...

I hope you enjoy!

book!!

Susan Ferrier

BLESSED BEYOND WORDS

Susan Ferrari

Bloomington, IN Milton Keynes, UK

AuthorHouse™
1663 Liberty Drive, Suite 200
Bloomington, IN 47403
www.authorhouse.com
Phone: 1-800-839-8640

AuthorHouse™ UK Ltd.
500 Avebury Boulevard
Central Milton Keynes, MK9 2BE
www.authorhouse.co.uk
Phone: 08001974150

First published by AuthorHouse 4/25/2006

ISBN: 1-4259-3127-8 (sc)

*Printed in the United States of America
Bloomington, Indiana*

This book is printed on acid-free paper.

Dedicated to Fred, Freddy, & TJ

**Family and friends who inspired
"Blessed Beyond Words"**

Alyssa, Angela, Anne, Anna, Anthony, Arminé, Barry, Cara, Casey Matthew, Catherine, Cole, Debbie, Eddie, Elizabeth, Fred Sr., Genevieve, Gianna, Hank, Jack, Janine, Jimmy, Joey, John, Johnny, Karen, Kathy, Lauren, Lorraine, Louis, Luigi, Mary Ellen, Mary, Matthew, Michael, Monsignor Wiest, Nancy, Nicholas, Nora, Pam, Peggy, Rob, Ronnie, Rosalie, Rosemarie, Ryan, Sally, Sheri, Susan, Terry, Theresa, and Tom

1

Adversity:
When life takes a 180 degree turn…

THE DAY I was diagnosed with renal cell carcinoma, I was practically in shock. My sister in law, who had accompanied me to my appointment, turned to me and said, "Wow, Sue, you really took the news quite well." What she didn't realize was that I was just so blown away that I couldn't express any emotions. I had no sadness, fear, or grief. Just disbelief. Yet I knew exactly why she thought I had taken it well; I had always taken everything well. That's me, the Queen of Positive Thinking.

I had spent my life thinking happy thoughts and encouraging others to do the same. I had always felt that I was blessed, and believed that everything would work out the way it should. "Everything happens for a reason," was my personal mantra. So why was this happening?

***

I had known for months that there was something wrong, but finding out what it was hadn't been easy. I had told friends of mine that I felt there was something inside of me that needed to come out. At the time, I ran a market research firm and was a mother of two boys, five years old and seven years old, while also dealing with the hassles of moving into a new home. My primary care physician related my symptoms to the stress I was currently undergoing, but I knew it was more than that.

I remember being in the car with my husband Fred on our way to a weekend vacation, when I asked him to turn around and take me to the emergency room. His response was "Not again...the doctors told you you're fine...there's nothing wrong with you." Well, Fred took me to the emergency room anyway. They did a full work up on me, to no avail. They found I was perfectly fine and released me several hours later, after giving me a heavy duty pain medication. At the time, I felt like I had been run over by a truck. I had pain in my head and in my back and basically everywhere.

Though I have the utmost respect for the medical field, I feel more accountable for my health than any doctor. I mean, after all, who knows my body better than me? And my body was telling me that something was very wrong. I've always believed in following my instincts, and I was determined to find out what was causing my pain.

So I continued to visit doctors, looking for an answer. I was tested for lyme disease, given several blood tests and x-rays, and nothing was showing up. Despite the inconclusive tests, I still believed something was wrong.

I told my doctor, "If I didn't know better, I'd think I was dying."

He looked at me almost as if to say, "Don't be ridiculous, you're not dying, you're young and healthy." This doctor thought it was all in my head, but I knew it wasn't. One thing is for sure, you always have to listen to your body.

Finally, something showed up! I was diagnosed with a urinary tract infection. I told my OB/GYN that I hadn't been feeling well and he told me the urinary tract infection could give you symptoms like the ones I had been experiencing. He prescribed me an antibiotic called Floxin, but after almost two weeks on the medication, I still wasn't feeling right. Deep down, I knew that the UTI wasn't the cause of my problems. Only a few days after I completed my antibiotic, I decided to call my orthopedic surgeon.

Looking back, I couldn't tell you exactly why I went to an orthopedic surgeon, I mean, who would think to go to an orthopedic surgeon with my symptoms? But I just had a strong intuitive feeling that Dr. Barry Fisher was going to help me find the problem. Dr. Barry had diagnosed previous illnesses in our family, and I knew if anyone could help me, it would be him. Dr. Barry decided to run an MRI and told the technician to get a shot of my right kidney. By just looking at me, Dr. Barry decided he wanted to rule out a renal tumor!

How did he know? There it was, a tumor of over four centimeters. Kidney cancer. It had to be removed immediately. Dr. Barry is definitely gifted in the area of diagnosing illness.

If something didn't tell me to see Dr. Barry, then I very well could have gone misdiagnosed until the cancer got worse and metastasized. If I had listened to those first doctors and ignored what my body was telling me, it could have been too late, perhaps too far gone to have saved my life. My whole point is that you must follow your instincts and listen to your inner voice. It might not make complete sense at the time, but in the long run, it all works out the way it should. This is a belief I've held my whole life, and that visit to Dr. Barry's office helped me confirm that I was on the right path.

After my diagnosis, I was forced to let go of many employees in my market research firm. I knew that this was the time I needed to take to focus on getting well. My business quickly became low on the totem pole as far as priorities. I had to devote this time to myself and my family. I remember knowing that whatever the outcome, everything was to turn out the way it should. I dreaded the idea of my husband and my two boys, Freddy and TJ, losing me. So many thoughts ran through my head but what I focused on was trying to keep a somewhat normal household, knowing full well that I may not be around to watch my children grow up or enjoy the golden years with my soul mate, Fred.

I knew I couldn't dwell on these thoughts; I had to be strong for my family. Fear was of no use to me and it definitely wasn't going to help me get better. I realized that fear is a pointless emotion. It may be a natural reaction to many situations, but it isn't helpful. I guess fear stems from the "what ifs" in life. What if something terrible happens? What if I lock my keys in the car? What if I miss the train? A "what if" isn't reality; it's the idea of something that hasn't happened, and may never happen. Why get worked up over something that isn't real? We have to remember we have no control over these situations. Things happen for a reason, and you can't stop something by worrying about it. All you can do is deal with an event when it occurs, you can't fix something that hasn't happened yet. Too many times we get caught up in the thoughts of what's to come, when all of our energies would be put to better use if we just enjoyed what we have at the moment. Sometimes the road ahead is rocky, but you must believe that whatever life brings you, you will endure. When good times are here, we must relish them and not take them for granted. It is in this moment that we live, not in the past or in the future. We must be thankful for what we have now, and enjoy it, because one never knows what tomorrow will bring. So why worry about it? Why be afraid of something that might never come to be?

While I knew there was no point in worrying about the future, I did feel a need to plan for the eventuality that my illness might get worse. In a strange way, I felt like I was being given the opportunity to prepare my family for life without me. Knowing that I may not live as long as I would have liked made me realize what things were truly important. I began to write down everything I would want my children and husband to know, in case I wasn't around to tell them. What follows are my letters.

***

Boys, be happy, because that's the only way to be. When life gets you down, think of everything around you that makes it worth living. Strive for success, that is, your own personal success. Remember, your success is based on you and you alone; it's your happiness that will guide you.

Listen to your heart, always. Though at times we all do the "wrong" thing, remember that what is right for someone else might not be what is right for you. Think about the big picture. Be creative, think outside the box. Remember, in life, sometimes you will be faced with decisions that are very hard and you have to remember the decision has to ALWAYS feel right even if you know it might not be a decision that everyone agrees on. Sometimes, when push comes to shove, you will feel like you are the only one standing. Your integrity is EVERYTHING. Never sacrifice your own integrity for anything or anyone. You have to live with yourself, everyday.

You can be whoever you want to be, it's up to you to make it happen, no one else. As life unfolds for you, reach for the stars, your possibilities are endless. You can endure the pain and suffering that you may face throughout your life, as long as you remember life's wonderful reasons for living. Each and every day, love like you never loved before, live like you never lived before, give like you never gave before, and you will receive all life's rewards.

If you don't learn to live, you won't! Tell those around you how you feel about them, because you never know when you will have the opportunity to tell them again. Though life is incredibly wonderful, it is very temporary and it's your turn, NOW, to make it the best it can be!

Strive to be the best you are instead of striving to be something you're not. Enjoy who you are even though at times, what you see is not necessarily what you like. Learn to love yourself and you will love others ten fold! And by loving others you will receive so much in return.

And last but not least, I love you with all my heart and soul and I know you feel the same! Don't feel guilty for the times I am not with you, but think of me often and with happy thoughts. Keep your chins up and shoot for the moon!

Now, for my husband. This is so difficult. I'm brought to tears! Well, we had it all, just like Bogey and Bacall! You know what's funny? There was never any other option for either of us. We wouldn't settle for any less than having it all.

We had laughter, we had romance, we had incredible intimacy, and we had beautiful children.

We had an incredible language between us that only we spoke. We found joy in each other's joy; we also found pain in each other's pain. We had the ability to overcome any situation, good or bad, even death. Through life and death, we will endure because the love we had for each other was endless and now I truly know the definition of eternal love.

My dear, you were truly a blessing in my life. You will endure. Whatever life has left to bring you, I know you will make the best of it. You always did. You are as strong as a lion and the integrity that you will continue to uphold is what makes you who you are. Be strong, my dear, I know that whatever you do, I will always be in your heart, until we meet again! Our love was our biggest gift of all.

To have loved and lost is truly better than never having loved at all! Keep smiling, my dear.

***

Shortly after my diagnosis, I was driving in my car, thinking about all the things I wanted to tell my children, and all the things I wanted them to know in case I wasn't around to watch them grow up. I wrote a song in my head, with all the lyrics. I felt as if I could hear a band playing around me! It was incredible; it literally took me five minutes to think up. When I got home I scribbled it on a piece of loose-leaf paper and sang it to them that night. They loved it! They made me sing it to them over and over again until they fell asleep. A while after I wrote it, I sang it to a friend of mine who loved it. She told me her father was a professional composer, and he met with me to arrange the music that I had been writing in my head!

Now, more than one year later, my children still ask me to sing the song to them every night at bedtime. Needless to say, they know the lyrics and the tune by heart. This song was my special message to them. It encompasses everything I wanted my children to know in an upbeat, inspirational melody. My hope is that the song inspires people to know that those who have passed before them are still with them in spirit.

***

- Your Guardian Angel -
I am the warmth in your sunshine
I am the twinkle in your eye
I am the voice in your laughter
It is through you I live my life
I am the answer to your prayer
I am the gaze within your stare
I'll be forever in your heart
And this way, we'll never be apart
I am the warmth in your sunshine
I am the twinkle in your eye
I am the voice in your laughter
It is through you I live my life
I am the pillow on which you rest
And I only wish you the best
Together we'll always be
Though I am someone you cannot see

It's time to hold your head up high
Don't let your faith just go awry
Keep up your prayers throughout your days
And they'll be answered in so many ways
I am the smile upon your face
I am the feelings in your joy
I am the good news in your days
I am those memories you cannot erase
In time your hearts will mend and
Your sadness will come to an end
We'll be seeing each other again
It will just be in heaven. Amen!

***

Since the day I was diagnosed with cancer, I've been determined to live my life to its fullest and appreciate the time I have. Whether I live for another year or another fifty years, I'm going to make every day count. I've felt blessed my entire life, and this certainly doesn't change anything!

People are constantly astounded by my outlook on life. They see how joyful I am, and often question how it's possible. A friend of mine once asked me how I could be so happy all the time. I just took one look at her and responded, "I don't quite think you understand, I am just thankful for every breath I take." I'm not happy every single minute of the day. Far from it! But I've learned how to cope with things. Sometimes you can't change a situation, but you can change your attitude towards it. Instead of being angry or fearful or sad, you have to look to all the other things in life that make you glad to be alive. I'm still realistic, though. I know life can be hard, and I know there are lots of people out there who get so bogged down by the hardships in life that they can't see all the good there is.

I hope that with this book, I can help some of those people. Dealing with cancer has shown me that I can get through even the most difficult situations, and I want to share that message with the world. I want to show you that life has a way of working itself out for the best, and you just have to hang on and enjoy the ride.

2

<u>Children:</u>
The greatest gift you can give a child is a childhood

THROUGH IT ALL, my children have been an incredible inspiration for me. Their love drives me to do my best every day, because I want to set a good example for them. They make me want to be strong and healthy so I can be here to share my love with them. They are truly my little miracles.

With my first-born, I had many complications during my pregnancy. I was about one month into my pregnancy when the morning sickness began; it ended up being afternoon sickness and evening sickness as well. I pretty much was sick throughout the whole day, everyday. Happy, ecstatic, but physically ill.

My body did not take well to being pregnant. In fact, during my pregnancy, I ended up in three different hospitals for three different reasons. At about five months, I experienced severe pain in my big, pregnant belly and woke my husband up to take me to the hospital. Fred had said, "Sue, you're fine, it's probably indigestion. Go back to sleep." I tried to wait it out, but when I went to go to the bathroom I could barely stand up straight from the pain. Finally, Fred spoke to my OB/GYN and drove me to over to the hospital. They did many tests and thought I had placenta previa, which is a condition in which the placenta covers the opening of the cervix and causes internal bleeding. I was immediately put on an IV and spent the night at the hospital. The pain eventually subsided and I was released and told to take it easy. So I did.

Well, despite following doctor's orders, that wasn't the end of it. I was later diagnosed with gestational diabetes. I was exactly two months away from giving birth when I ended up in the hospital, in what they called pre-term labor. I was there for a few days while they gave me medication to stop the labor. I was then released and put on strict bed rest. I was allowed to go to the bathroom and back but was required to stay in a lying down position the rest of the time. Well, needless to say, I did just that. Everyone who called and came to visit couldn't believe my high-spirited attitude. I was about to give birth to my first son, how could I have felt otherwise! Friends and relatives kept telling me how well I was taking the whole situation and how I was so patient. What most didn't realize is that when you're going through struggles in your life or health issues, you have no choice but to keep your head up. The way I see it, there's only one zone you can live in and that's the positive zone. If you're not living in the positive zone, you're not living! Despite my health issues, I had everything in the world to be happy about. I was about to have a son! I had no idea that I still had more difficulties ahead, though.

One of my last visits to my OB/GYN was somewhat alarming. My doctor took my blood pressure and my pulse, and sent me right over to St. Francis Hospital. Now, keep in mind, St. Francis Hospital is a heart hospital, not a baby hospital! My husband, who had to fly home early from a business meeting in Chicago, took a look at me and at the person next to me and said, "Boy, that guy's in really bad shape, his heart rate is only 67." At the time, mine was fluctuating between 130 and 140 beats per minute. It didn't dawn on Fred that 67 was the normal heart rate and that I was the one in really bad shape! Sometimes when it comes to our loved ones being sick, our coping mechanisms kick in and we go into a stage of denial! I was admitted for a few days and the doctors couldn't seem to get my heart rate down to normal. They basically blamed it on the stress my body undergoes while pregnant. I was suffering from a condition called tachacardia which is when your heart rate is persistently too high. Eventually, my heart rate went down to normal range and I was released to go back on bed rest. At my very last doctor's visit, which was only six days before my due date, I went for a sonogram and the sonographer called my doctor and told him to go to the hospital immediately because my amniotic fluid was dangerously low. They attempted to induce labor, but after hours of trying to give birth, the doctors performed a c-section because of failure to progress. I had a very slow recovery from the c-section. I remember not being able to walk for about the first two weeks after Freddy was born. Thankfully, the baby was healthy and it was truly a miraculous event to give birth to my first son, Freddy.

***

One day when Freddy was about a year old, I was lying side by side with my husband on the sofa, watching TV and chatting. Fred asked me if maybe we should start thinking about having a second child. We always imagined our children to be close in age so that they could play with each other and have a close relationship, you know, so they would have more things in common. Well, at that very moment, I said to Fred, "I'll be right back," and I ran to the local drug store. I brought back a home pregnancy test to see if I was pregnant . . . and I was! Most people would call it a coincidence, but I think these types of things are meant to be. Everything happens for a reason, and if your inner voice tells you something, you should listen! I had a gut feeling that there was another baby on the way! The timing was perfect! The second pregnancy wasn't easy on me either, but once again, I gave birth to a beautiful, healthy baby boy.

I always planned on having a large family, but sometimes things don't work out the way we expect them to. After two very difficult pregnancies that compromised my health, my doctor advised me to stop at two. Needless to say, I was extremely upset. My attitude was, "So what if I have to stay in bed for months?" and "So what if my body doesn't take well to being pregnant?" It seemed like it would only be a temporary setback, and it was a very small sacrifice to make in exchange for the blessing of children. Well, the doctor informed me that it was a "miracle" that we even conceived my second son, TJ. A large amount of scar tissue had formed from my first pregnancy, in addition to the fibroids, endometriosis, gestational diabetes, tachacardia, and the placenta previa. I was loaded with high-risk conditions. He basically told me that what I had were two blessings and that would be it! I would be unable to have any more children.

It wasn't easy news to take, and I was definitely disappointed. Then I stopped feeling sorry for myself and thought about what he had said. With all my health problems, it really was a miracle that I was able to conceive two children. Despite all the problems, I lived through two incredibly difficult pregnancies, and gave birth to two healthy baby boys. Why be sad about something I couldn't have, when I had something amazing right in front of me? I now realize the doctor was right, and I see how blessed I am with my two beautiful boys!

Talk about life's most precious gift! It's all about children! Children truly light up the world around us. As an adult, you can easily get caught up in the humdrum of life's existence. Then a child greets you or gives you a hug, and the purity of their love and affection makes you forget all your worries. There are some things in life you just can't buy, and a child's love is absolutely at the top of the list.

Having children helps remind us of what's important. They help us to see the true meaning of life. Through their innocence, they show us what life can be like without the worries and hassles we face every day. They follow their instincts without question, and aren't compromised by the pressures and prejudices of the world. There is often great wisdom in a child's words, and we would all be better off if we paid attention.

A while back, my son Freddy spilled his glass of milk all over the kitchen table. He looked at the milk, and then at me, and said, without a moment's hesitation, "Mommy you shouldn't cry over spilled milk!" It's an old saying, but one we take for granted. As adults, when we spill that milk, we often forget what's important. All we can do is look at the runny mess on the floor and cry about it. Whether the spilled milk is forgetting a friend's birthday or doing poorly on a job interview, it's something we can't go back and redo. Spilled milk is everything and anything that is in our past that we cannot change! We have to pick up a towel, wipe up the mess and move on. You can't change what happened, you have to deal with it the best you can and keep going. This made perfect sense to my son. Why should he cry over the milk when he has so much love and happiness in his life? It's just milk, he'll get over it, and Mommy should, too!

My younger son TJ is every bit as insightful. Back when he was in preschool, the class was learning about Christopher Columbus day. The teacher told them how people used to believe the world was flat, but Columbus discovered it was round. TJ raised his hand and told the teacher, "Mrs. Duncan, I know what makes the world go around!"

Mrs. Duncan asked, "What's that, TJ?"

"Love!" Right then and there, I knew I did my job as a mother. It brought tears to my eyes to hear Mrs. Duncan retell the story from class that day.

It's funny, the hardest part of motherhood is not teaching your children how to make the bed, how to dress themselves, or how to read. It's figuring out how to teach them to be good people with the world the way it is. It's so hard to explain why an airplane flew into a building and killed thousands, or why people turn guns on each other all the time! A child's mind can't comprehend the vast array of thoughts and emotions that we experience as adults. How do you interpret horrific happenings to a five year old when you barely understand them yourself?

It's a struggle to convince them of their safety when you don't feel that secure or comfortable yourself. We need to hold up those protective walls we build for them, even if our own walls have fallen. There are no guarantees in life, but we still need to help our children believe that things will be O.K. If they see that we're secure, they will feel the same. As long as we believe that things will work themselves out and we can get through whatever hardships come our way, we can stay strong for our children. Faith is a gift that we can help instill in our children at a very young age.

Parenting is a total sacrifice of oneself because our very existence is enveloped by our children; we live for them. Our lives are all about ensuring their safety, their health, their happiness and their love! By giving our hearts to our children so completely, we can teach them a valuable lesson about being good to others. We can show them that even though there may be bad people in the world, we all have the ability to be kind and loving. We will be their example.

A close friend of mine once shared with me that she thought I was bringing up my children in a bubble, and that I need to teach them what the "real world" is all about. She felt I was setting my children up for a rude awakening. My first thought was, "No, my friend, I need to teach them what the real world should be about." The real world should be filled with people who have respect and compassion for one another. The real world should be filled with a sense of gratitude for the little things life brings us. That's what I try to instill in my children. I give them the tools to become loving to their neighbor no matter how horrible people can be sometimes. I don't feel the need to tell my children that the world is a hard and mean place. Some people want to raise their kids to think that life is a battle and they must fight their way through. I don't think that's productive. I show my children how to be kind and caring, and how to deal with the obstacles that come their way, and I know they will be just fine.

I believe that teaching by example is one of the most effective ways to raise children. We, as parents, cannot force our children to be what they are not. Children are like plants that we water, and not like sculptures we mold. We can only feed our children all the right ideas and provide a good example. We can't make them be who we want them to be.

As a mother, I can see how children would turn to alcohol or drugs, or be rebellious in other ways. There are not enough parents in the world who really tell their children, "It's O.K. just to be you." I pray for parents today that they let their children be children, and let them grow instead of trying to sculpt them. Some parents push their children and force their path, whether it's right for the kids or not. These children want to be free to be themselves; they don't want to be their parents! Of course they're going to rebel against the ideas their parents force on them! For the most part, I think every parent's hope is merely their children's happiness, and it's important to understand that what makes us happy will not necessarily make our children happy. Our children are separate and distinct individuals with their own thoughts, ideas and desires. They have their own personalities which may be very different from our own. What works for us will not always work for them. Give them the tools they need to be a good person, but don't try and tell them how they should live.

I once saw a sign in a store window that said, "The best gift you can give a child is a childhood." Wow, what a concept! As parents, we assume we are giving our children a childhood, but look at all the pressure we put on them day in and day out. Being a kid can be much more stressful than we realize! Imagine, for a moment, having to follow all kinds of rules every day that you don't even understand. Imagine having to live by someone else's schedule, with no idea why things are happening or what's expected of you. Children don't understand the demands of our daily lives, yet they constantly feel the effects. We have to remember that our burdens are not our children's burdens. They shouldn't have to deal with the stresses that we do.

Taking time to let your children play for a little while every day is so crucial to their childhood experience. Before you know it, their childhood will be gone and they'll be off to college. We have about eighteen years to build wonderful memories so that our children can look back with enjoyment on their early years. It's so important to let them be silly and express themselves freely. Letting them take the time to be kids gives them a chance to find out who they really are. It gives them the opportunity to be themselves, free of expectations; it encourages their individuality and creativity. We have to let them embrace their own personality and accept that we can't change who they are. Their lives shouldn't be dictated by how we want them to act.

Every year, at the end of the school year, I hold an end of the year celebration party at our home. Year after year, people would come to our gathering, saying things like, "Wow, I can't believe you're having this party, that's so nice of you." For me, it was just a way to let my kids have a little fun after a hard year of schoolwork.

One little girl named Charlotte said to me after the first day of school last year, "Even though I'm not in Freddy's class, can I still be invited to the end of the year party?" Now, keep in mind, when she asked me, the year had barely even started; there was more than 250 days to go before the party!

Of course, my response was, "You'll always be invited!"

Before the annual end of the school year party, one mother asked me, "What are the kids going to do, what do you have planned?"

I just looked at her and said, "Well, I figure they'll be hungry, so we'll feed them, and if they get hot, they can run through the sprinkler." Now it doesn't get simpler than that, does it? The party was to celebrate being done with school, I thought the kids should be free to play and have fun without a schedule! I didn't want to impose certain activities on them; they're kids, and they'll make their own fun! And you know what, after the party, that little girl Charlotte told me it was the best party she had ever attended. I believe the adults had a nice time, too.

***

I remember when my youngest son, TJ, was discovering his artistic ability. We had just refinished the basement and we decided on white textured wallpaper for all the walls in the room. Well, lo and behold, TJ found a purple crayon and drew a picture for Mommy on the wallpaper, instead of on loose-leaf paper. He must have been all of four years old, if that. As soon as he finished his masterpiece, he called for me. "Mommy, Mommy, come quick, I made you something!" Hearing his enthusiastic voice, I ran down to see what all the excitement was about. It took every bit of my self-control not to scream!

I stopped and thought for a very brief moment and looked at my son, who was so proud of his Picasso. I said to him, in all sincerity, "Oh, TJ, it's absolutely beautiful, did you do that all by yourself?"

He responded with a big, proud smile, "Yep, Mommy, ALL by myself . . . isn't it beautiful?!"

I very patiently said to him, "Oh, it's really beautiful. Maybe next time you could do it on drawing paper instead of on the wall, O.K. honey?"

Here he was, incredibly proud of what he did, expressing his artistic ability, and he was so thrilled to share it with me. Now, there I was, about to blow a gasket! I was able to calm myself down and see it from his point of view. To him, paper was paper! No one had explained to him that the paper on the wall wasn't used for drawing on like paper in notebooks. He wanted to make me a gift, and I'm sure the wall seemed like a wonderful place to display it. I knew that this was a genuine show of affection, and not an attempt to be rebellious or troublesome. He was expressing himself to me in a way that made sense to him. How could I be angry at him for that? So I thanked him for his efforts, and calmly explained to him that wallpaper is not for drawing on. Needless to say, it never happened again!

It's so important we don't crush our children's spirits. As parents, we have to handle many situations with an understanding of where children are coming from. If I had yelled at TJ, or punished him for drawing on the wall, I might have stifled his creativity. He wouldn't have understood why he was being yelled at and he would probably have thought that I didn't appreciate the gift he had made for me. When children express themselves in ways we don't like we need to understand that their intentions are often good, even if they're somewhat misguided.

For instance, Freddy, my oldest son, decided to clean his room and organize his desk the other day. Well, that was all wonderful; however, he had about two hours of homework to complete. He was in there until about 8 p.m., and I assumed he was doing his homework. Well, I was wrong. He came out of his room and said, "Mommy, come see what I did!" He even made his brother's bed! Unfortunately, this time, instead of acknowledging the wonderful job he did, I simply lost it.

"What are you doing cleaning your room when you have two hours of homework ahead of you and you still need to shower and go to bed!?"

Well, his face dropped and he said back to me with a scowl, "Fine, I'll get my homework done!" Obviously I was a little cranky that he was running behind and I knew that to finish his homework, he'd have to stay up about two hours past his bedtime. After he fell asleep, and the dust settled, I realized that I had handled it the wrong way.

At the time, I felt he should have made the choice to clean up after his homework was done, since homework was the top priority. He told me he felt better working in a neat and organized environment. Mind you, he's only ten years old. Well, I didn't consider his position whatsoever and I ended up hurting his feelings after he worked so hard to accomplish something. I knew that I should have been thankful that I have a son who would clean his room without being told, and who considers cleanliness to be an important thing.

Now I had to figure out how to repair the damage. The next morning, I woke him up and said to him, "I'm sorry I was a little short with you last night, but as your mother, I was quite concerned about you getting to bed on time. Freddy, I want you to know, you did an awesome job cleaning your room and organizing your desk!"

I couldn't let the moment go by without him hearing me say these words. It was very important to let him know that I was appreciative of his accomplishment. The night before, I had been so worried about him getting his homework done and getting to sleep that I didn't even think about what a great child he was for cleaning up his room. It was crucial that I acknowledge his initiative, and apologize for snapping at him. I wanted him to realize that I'm only human and far from perfect, just like everyone else, but that when we make mistakes, we should admit to them and try to correct them. I showed him that apologizing is a very big part of good communication.

Children absorb so much from us, even when we don't realize it. They're very in tune with our feelings and reactions, and it's important that we're always aware of that. Have you ever noticed that when a small child falls down, they look around before they react? If you get upset, they'll start to cry. But often, if you react calmly, or laugh it off, you can prevent the tears. Children can tell when we're upset or angry. Keeping a positive outlook on life will help your child in immeasurable ways.

If you run into problems with your children, getting angry and frustrated can be the natural reaction. It's not a productive one, though! Positive reinforcement works wonders. Have faith in your children and they'll respond to your encouragement.

I was speaking to a mother today that brought up a very valid point. She mentioned that one of her sons was a pretty difficult child in respect to school performance and behavior. She said confidently, in the same breath, that it was nothing that she did wrong. Now, someone who overheard her would probably think, "How did you let your son go awry?" or "Why didn't you do something to help him?" Well, neither of those were the case in her scenario. She tried, but to no avail. She had done everything she could to help and encourage her son. Everyone in the school had lost hope that her son would ever graduate with his class. He needed an 87% on his English regents to pass. No one believed he could do it, except for his mother.

Well, lo and behold, he received an 87% EXACTLY! He did it because his mother never lost hope; she kept her faith in him. He is now attending a school down in Florida and he's actually attaining A's! By believing in her son, she gave him the strength to keep trying. If he had felt that everyone, even his mother, had given up on him, what motivation would he have to succeed? With his mother cheering him on, he graduated when no one thought he could.

It can be difficult to find the right balance between encouraging your children and pressuring them. You want to motivate them without pushing them. Kids won't always get A's in school, even if they work hard and study. They're not always going to be perfect, but that doesn't mean they're not trying.

The other day, we came home from my son Freddy's basketball game. He plays with a bunch of his friends on a local team. He came home rather discouraged, and I assumed it was because he lost the game 49 – 8. He actually wasn't that upset over the score. What bothered him was that his teammates were so competitive that they were putting their other teammates down. What Freddy realized is that it's just not worth the pressure of winning. It's a game. It's supposed to be fun! Well, unfortunately, the team doesn't have what one would call good teamwork; some of them are just out to win and some of them simply give up if they are losing by too much of a margin. I told Freddy to keep his chin up and not to worry. I said that the more the team practices, the more they will come together as friends and teammates. It's interesting that at the age of ten, these children are so pressured to win. Coaches these days are out for blood instead of teaching kids the fun of the sport. Instead of teaching sportsmanlike conduct, they constantly yell at the children to do better. Freddy's right, is it really worth it?

Give your children the chance to enjoy life without unneeded pressures. They only have a few years before they have to enter the adult world and deal with the stresses that you face every day. Allow them to have this time to be happy and innocent. It can be hard to sit back and not worry, to give them the freedom to be kids, without agonizing over what could go wrong.

The other day at a children's party, one of the mothers mentioned to me that when she became a parent, she thought her only worries were going to be to make sure she could provide for her children, keep them clothed and fed and just give them plenty of love. Now, in today's world, we have to think every step of the way. Where are they? Who are they with? What are they doing? How are they feeling? What are their fears? I guess it's just a sign of the times. It's not like when we were kids, and we could run free in the streets, with the world as our oyster. But as parents today, we have different alternatives, like getting our children involved in extra curricular activities. You can nurture their creativity in a number of ways through extra curricular activities. Or, then again, you can do what I do and let them be kids and play at home a lot! There are plenty of ways to keep your children safe and happy, without having to worry about where they are. Your children will appreciate being given the chance to pursue their interests and make new friends, and you can relax knowing that they're in a safe, organized activity.

It's so important to listen to your children and be in touch with their interests and feelings. As I said earlier, you can't mold a child to be who you want them to be. You have to be aware of their personality, and encourage them to be themselves. It's amazing what you can learn if you really listen.

My son Freddy had a rocky start in first grade. Most parents would have waited until the end of the school year in hopes of a better following year; you know, grin and bear it. Not I! Life is too short not to be happy, and it was very clear to me that Freddy was not happy. I couldn't fathom a six year old disliking school as much as Freddy did. Now, I know a lot of people would say, "Kids just don't like school, that's the way it is!" but I knew this was not normal. This was more than complaints about homework and waking up early!

I literally did not let another day go by with my son being unhappy. We ended up sending him to a nearby Catholic school. At this point, school was only in session for a little over two months. When we broke the news to Freddy that he would be changing schools, he was ecstatic. Incredibly, a few days earlier, a girl happened to leave this school and so there was a spot that opened up for my son. I truly believe everything happens for a reason! He was able to start school in the class we had hoped for. Simply put, it was meant to be. Needless to say, Freddy had a great teacher and a great year. I knew deep down that changing his school was the right choice, and the only option. I listened to my instincts when they told me to act. He's so much happier now, and I know it meant a lot to him that we paid attention to his feelings.

There's an interesting side note to this story. As Freddy began enjoying his new school, my husband started thinking about moving closer to Freddy's school. Fred, my husband, felt that where we lived was too far for Freddy to commute. I had absolutely no interest in moving, but Fred began to speak to his mother about finding a place in Manhasset, closer to the school. Fred's mother works for a realtor in that area and she faxed us over some listings of houses we might be interested in. Among those listings was the very house that Fred grew up in! This house had been occupied by another family for over twenty years, and it just so happened to go back on the market at the same time we were looking! Now, a year later, I still can't believe I'm here! I absolutely love it in Manhasset. When I think about the chain of events that brought us here, it's astounding. By paying attention to my son's concerns, and switching his school, my family has ended up living in the very house where my husband grew up. It's such a wonderful feeling to be surrounded by this sense of history and family in our home. Again, it was just meant to be!

I feel so blessed that my sons can share in the joy that my husband experienced growing up in this home. Being in this home helps them understand their roots and feel connected to their family's past, and family is so important.

I feel one of the greatest gift you can give a child is a sibling. It's a mother's job to teach her children how precious their sisters and brothers are and to always treat them with tender care and understanding. I make it a conscious effort to remind them day in and day out how blessed they are to have each other. I believe having a sibling teaches you so much about being caring and compassionate. It gives a child the chance to learn from an early age how to coexist with another person. Interacting with a brother or sister teaches a child more than they could ever learn from just being around their parents. Parents are authority figures and adults, but siblings are equals, someone on the same level. With proper parental guidance, having a sibling can provide invaluable lessons on being sympathetic, kind, and tolerant. More than that, it gives a child someone to play with when parents are busy or exhausted. A sibling is a friend and a partner, and an incredible blessing to have.

This is something I like to talk about in the religious education class I teach for 4th graders. I tell the students that we are here to make the world a better place, and that means caring for all of God's creations, especially other people! We must teach children to care not only for their family and siblings, but for their friends, neighbors, and the less fortunate. My job during these classes is to teach the children, but more often than not, I find they are teaching me!

We spoke about the soul in class once, and one little girl said to me, "I know what a soul is, it's that something that's alive inside us." Another little boy answered, "It's what makes us who we are." Now, these were responses that came out of the mouths of nine year olds! I was pretty impressed to hear how insightful they are. I remember when I was nine years old, I thought a soul was my favorite fish or a type of music!

As I said before, children can show us so much. These 4th graders taught me that you're never too young to have faith. I realized that children do understand the lessons we're trying to teach them, even if they only comprehend it on a simpler level. Kids soak up everything around them, so take the time to make sure you're giving them a positive example to learn from.

3

<u>Love & Marriage:</u>
As long as you believe...life is all about timing

I REMEMBER THE day I told my husband I was pregnant with our first son. We were just married and didn't have two nickels to rub together. We moved into a new home that we purchased together and had no furniture, just a bunch of cardboard boxes. Before we got married, Fred lived with his parents and I lived with mine. We saved up all our money so that we could buy a house. Both Fred and I were going to have to work to keep up with the new bills we were going to have as homeowners.

When I got home from our honeymoon, I visited my OB/GYN to discuss birth control. The doctor took a urine sample and came back into the room and said, "Well, we will not be discussing birth control today."

I looked at him puzzled and asked "Why not?"

He looked back at me and said, "Because there's no need to discuss it, you're pregnant." It turns out I got pregnant on our honeymoon without realizing it or intending to. I had one of those out of body experiences where you feel like you're watching someone else in a movie instead of actually living your life. I just couldn't believe it. After a few seconds, a smile came over my face and I became instantly ecstatic.

However, when I sat Fred down to share the good news, his reaction wasn't exactly what I had hoped for. I knew it wasn't the ideal time to tell Fred I was pregnant, but I had no choice. There was no turning back. Not only had we just begun to share our life together, now we had to deal with the fact that we were going to become parents before our one year wedding anniversary!

When I told him, his response was to scream, "What?! We just got married! We have no money! How could this happen!?" Well, needless to say, my eyes welled up with tears. I knew our situation wasn't ideal, but I had hoped he'd be happier about the news. After he composed himself, he hugged me and said, "I'm sorry. I'm happy...this just came out of left field." Here was a perfect example of a situation that was truly out of our control at that point. Sometimes life takes you on a journey that you weren't planning on taking. Instead of fighting it and making yourself miserable, you should accept that this is your path, and enjoy the ride. It happened and we had to go along with it, and to this day we are so happy we did! It turned out that if I did not get pregnant with my children when I did, if we had waited, there was most likely going to be no hope for us to have children, due to my medical complications.

You have to believe that timing is everything in life and that the timing of one event has a direct effect on the timing of all the other events that surround you and those you come in contact with. Nothing is by chance. When it happened, it seemed like the most inopportune time to have a baby. But looking back now, years later, it really was the absolute right time for everything in our lives to fall into place. I knew everything was going to work out, and it has.

We were able to get through this difficult time because of the incredible love and respect we have for each other. Fred and I have been through more together than the average couple. We've dealt with adversity and heartache, and we survived it all. No matter what lies ahead of us, we know we can face it together. On the same note, we've accomplished so much and enjoyed each other more than you could ever imagine. So far, it's a love affair that has lasted fifteen years and it's still going strong. When you have a meaningful, loving, healthy relationship, nothing affects it. The world could come tumbling down around you and you would still make it through. Is it easy? Absolutely not! Is it a struggle sometimes? Of course! But when you truly love each other, you make it through, no matter what! It is like an eternal flame that continues to burn as hot as ever, and never goes out. Healthy relationships do not get comfortable and routine, they just keep getting stronger. They're eternal, like a life long love affair. To death do you part, and then some! This is what Fred and I share. I really believe that we were brought together by fate.

Looking back on it now, it seems like something truly magical happened at our first meeting. My twin sister, Eve-lynn, introduced us at a bar called Marbles in Locust Valley, New York. I had gone to the bar with Eve-lynn, and she was really enjoying herself. I was ready to head out, though. It was getting late and all I wanted to do was to get home to bed! Well, at the very moment that I was about to tell my sister I wanted to leave, in walks one of Eve-lynn's old boyfriends with a friend of his. I thought to myself, "This night is never going to end!" I had just been getting ready to head out of there, and now Eve-lynn was chatting it up with her old beau Gary.

Eve-lynn saw the frustration in my face, so she asked Gary what his friend's name was. Eve-lynn actually took Gary's friend Fred by the hand and pulled him toward me. She knew this guy just as long as I had, about two minutes, and yet she introduced us as if he was an old friend. She said, "Fred, this is my sister Susan. Susan, this is Fred." Now, her whole thought pattern was, "If Fred just occupies Sue's time for a while, I can hang out a little longer." Well, I was so intrigued by Fred, I completely forgot about the guy I was dating at the time. I thought I liked him but after meeting Fred, he was a mere blip. I can't even remember his name!

So, there we were, about to leave Marbles after hours of having fun and dancing with my friends, and in walks Fred, a total stranger, and my twin sister introduces me to him! The timing was uncanny, but it was no coincidence. We were destined to meet. Our love was truly written by fate.

I knew from the very beginning that my love for Fred was undying. On our wedding day, I was, of course, extremely excited. Here I was, marrying the love of my life, and I wanted everything to be perfect! Just like any other bride, I had dreams of outdoor wedding pictures on a beautiful summer's day. It wasn't meant to be. What we got was a torrential downpour. It was every bride's nightmare; rain on your wedding day! But even though I knew it was going to be a bad hair day for all, it didn't matter one bit! On June 5, 1993, I realized it wasn't at all about the perfect wedding pictures and the flowers and the limousines and all the other incidentals we had spent a year preparing. It was about celebrating our love and uniting as one in marriage. In fact, after the ceremony, I was on such a cloud that nothing seemed to matter other than sharing this day with my husband and family and friends. What a celebration it was!

Perhaps the most amazing part of the day was when Monsignor Whelan performed the actual ceremony. We each took a lit candle and used them to light one bigger candle together, to symbolize our marriage union. As Monsignor Whelan spoke the words "One body," it was as if his words pierced our very beings and we could both feel our souls actually unite. I remember the look on Fred's face and how I felt at that very moment. It was almost as if the earth rumbled within us. Our marriage was blessed from that day forward.

My marriage is so wonderful that sometimes I wish I could just have the chance to prove to all the single people in the world that it is so worth waiting for the right person to come along. Unfortunately, the majority of people settle and some end up being nothing more than content. Some people think being content is good enough, but I've always believed, good enough isn't good enough! Why settle when you can have real happiness? It exists; I know it does, because I experience it every day! Unfortunately, some people settle because they believe that is the best they can hope for, and true love is only a fairy tale. If they only knew bliss really existed, I'm sure they would hold out.

Of course, the waiting can get lonely, and that's often why people marry the wrong person. They don't want to be alone anymore. But is spending your life with someone you don't truly love really any better than being alone? That's a perfect example of letting fear and "what ifs" motivate you. People sit there and say to themselves, "What if I never meet the right person? What if this is the best I'm going to find?" That's such a terrible way to go through life! You should only marry out of love, never out of fear of being alone.

If you took all the people you know who ever got divorced and asked both parties about their marriage, I guarantee at least one of them would admit that there was "something missing" or they had an inkling that things didn't feel completely right. Or they might say they knew there were problems but they hoped that their spouse would change over time. Why would you ever marry a person that you thought needed to change? You should love someone for who they are, and accept them with all their quirks. If you can't accept them, then you shouldn't be getting married.

I believe there is someone for everyone; however, too many people get married for the wrong reasons. Many women think about their biological clock when making decisions. They tell themselves they're running out of time and they better take what they can get. They marry the wrong person out of fear. These types of relationships never end well!

Think about what happens when people realize that they chose the wrong person to spend the rest of their life with. Some get divorced in hopes of finding Mr. or Mrs. Right. Some don't even bother to get divorced; they start searching for new love while they're married and end up having affairs. Others just settle and say to themselves, "I guess this is as good as it's going to get," and remain together for the sake of doing the "right" thing. We certainly don't want to judge anyone; everyone has to do what is right for them, and their situation. We can't know what it's like to live in someone else's shoes or know the challenges they have to face.

It's amazing how some people can be in a content marriage and think everything is wonderful, and then one day they meet that person who turns their world around and shows them how incredible love can really be. I truly believe you cannot be in love with your spouse, and then fall out of love because someone else comes along. There had to be something lacking in the relationship for a spouse to cheat. A spouse doesn't stray because of an attraction to another person; a spouse strays because they are not satisfied in their current relationship. Sometimes people manage to convince themselves that they're happy when they're really not, or maybe they simply don't know any better. When you've never experienced true love, it can be very easy to settle into a routine with someone and marry out of convenience. But if real love does happen to come along, it definitely throws a monkey wrench into things.

So if your husband or wife strays, what are you supposed to do? Many people accept it and stay, and many have affairs of their own. I say, leave the spouse. Why stay? Who are you staying for? You're not staying for yourself, how could you be happy in a relationship knowing your spouse doesn't truly love you? You're definitely not staying for your spouse. Why would your spouse want you to stay if they're in love with someone else?

What about the children? Should you decide to stay in a bad marriage for the sake of the children?

Well, a child looks at their parents' relationship to learn what marriage and love is all about. You're a role model for your children, and what you do sets an example for them and influences their lives. If you stay together, you're showing your children an unhealthy marriage. You're telling them that this behavior is O.K., and that this is how marriage is supposed to be. If this is what they grow up with, and what they believe to be true, they'll have a good chance of making the same mistake. There is nothing worse than bringing a child up in a home where the parents are not in love and do not show respect for each other.

Or you can show the children that this isn't the way marriage is supposed to be and you separate. It's very possible that they may become devastated, but it's also possible that they may not. It all depends on the severity of unhappiness in the marriage and how your particular relationship was. Sometimes it is even clear to the child that the decision to divorce could be a blessing in disguise. Especially with older children who have an easier time grasping the complex emotions involved, they may see that it's better for their parents to be happy separately than unhappy together. Eventually though, all children will grow up and understand your decision, but it can certainly take a while. My only advice in any of these scenarios is to follow your heart; it will always lead you in the right direction. This is much easier said than done. No one wants to hurt the people they love. It's not easy!!

It can be incredibly difficult to leave an unhappy marriage. Most people are afraid of having to start all over and be single again. Those same "what ifs" come back; "What if I never find anyone else? What if this is the best I can hope for?" You can't let "what ifs" stand in the way of reason, and you certainly can't let them stand in the way of your heart.

***

I have a friend name Janice who is a Special Education teacher at a local high school. She's a wonderful person, as you can imagine, since it takes a special, compassionate person to do the type of job she does. Janice had been married before I met her, but it didn't work out. She was twenty-one years old when they met. She was engaged to her first husband when she was twenty-two and married by age twenty-four. Janice was married for five years before they separated for the first time. During their separation her husband pursued her and promised that he would work hard at making their marriage better. She finally agreed to try again, but after eight months of being back together, Janice realized her marriage just wasn't going to work out. She tried to make it work, but she felt like she was just going through the motions. It was hard for her to admit failure. One day she looked over at him and said, "This is not what I want for the rest of my life." She felt like she was living a useless existence.

She never had a strong connection with her husband. Janice felt she was much more superficial when she was in her early twenties. She married a model, he was gorgeous and she figured she could make it work. Though they tried, through counseling, to make the marriage work, the counselor said to Janice, "You're dealing with a narcissist." The counselor recommended Janice get out of this unhealthy relationship.

While Janice and her husband were separated, Janice survived a severe car accident. She was hit by a car that was traveling about seventy miles an hour. The car that hit her did not stop, but the police found the car that hit her one mile away from the scene of the accident where it eventually gave out due to the damage from the impact. Janice was hit so hard that the force of the crash flipped her car over twice. While Janice was upside down, with her car spinning on its roof, another car came smashing into her. All the glass in her car shattered. There were no wheels remaining. Every single tire on the car had fallen off and they were found hundreds of feet away.

Her doctors couldn't quite understand how she even survived such a horrific accident. She was immediately knocked unconscious from the impact and suffered intestinal bleeding. She experienced a severe concussion, and developed hearing loss from the head trauma. She had water on the brain and suffered from amnesia. Doctors couldn't believe she had no facial injuries at all. . . there wasn't a scratch on her face!

Janice never saw the car coming. She recalls nothing other than being in the ambulance and hearing the words, "We're losing her." She later found out that one of her old high school students was an EMT on the ambulance.

Janice and her husband never got back together after her accident. She dealt with her injuries without him, and eventually they got a divorce. Obviously, this was a marriage that wasn't built on true love and respect. Anyone who's really been in love knows they would go to the ends of the earth to take care of their loved ones. It's terrible that Janice had to go through such a horrific event for her and her husband to realize their marriage wasn't working, but I think in the end, she was better off knowing the truth so she could move on with her life.

Eventually, she regained her health and began dating again. Janice's first relationship after her divorce was a restaurant owner named John. This lasted for a short while before she was told by one of his co-workers that John was having a relationship with another employee at the restaurant. Janice had suspected something was going on, but John had denied such allegations. Deep down, Janice knew that the relationship wasn't going to work. Eventually, she broke up with him. Then Janice met Stuart, who she dated for two years. Stuart was "fine", but after a while, "fine" just wasn't going to cut it. She ended this relationship, realizing it wasn't what she was looking for. She wanted more out of her life and knew that a relationship must feel right on all levels. It seemed like Janice had one relationship disappointment after another.

I would see Janice about once a week and I was always telling her to hold out for that one special person who makes her heart skip a beat. Well, knowing she'd never really experienced the actual feeling, she pretty much humored me by saying, "O.K. Sue, I'll hold out for that special someone." What I didn't realize was the whole time she really didn't believe there was someone like that for her. She dated here and there and had a couple of steady boyfriends but no one that truly made her happy. Content? Yes. Happy? No.

Well, something magical happened within one week in Janice's life. Janice sometimes works as a tutor and has clients in different towns near where she lives. A couple of days after Janice broke up with Stuart, the mother of one of Janice's students asked her, "So, how's your love life?" Janice thought the timing of the question was a bit funny, since she had just broken up with Stuart. Well, her client said, "I've got a guy for you, his name is Evan." Evan called Janice the very next day and asked her out on an early date for the following Sunday.

A day later, Janice's friend Ann mentioned to her, "I know my friend Tracy has a brother named Evan, maybe you should meet him?"

Janice, amused, said to Ann, "That's funny you should say that, he called me and we're getting together this Sunday."

The day after THAT, a friend named Liz said, "There's this guy I know named Evan. I think you should meet him." Janice couldn't believe her ears.

Three different people, who don't even know each other, recommended she meet Evan all in the same week! Now, keep in mind she just broke up with her boyfriend of two years only a couple of days ago.

Well, Janice met Evan on a Sunday in mid-May and honestly, she was not that interested in going on another date with him. However, because of the week of coincidences, she felt that she had to give it one more try. She asked herself, "What are the odds that three different people who don't even know each other refer me to this man in the very same week? There must be something to it."

Janice agreed to go on a second date with Evan on Memorial Day weekend. Lo and behold, Janice fell for Evan, hook, line and sinker. She felt that he was honest and trustworthy and she had a feeling deep down inside of her that this was it. After all the relationship trials and tribulations, Janice found what she was waiting for, after only two dates! Janice and Evan were engaged on August 17, only three months after they met. They married the following March 12th. Now, within less than one year of meeting, Janice is pregnant with their first baby. It's a boy!

Janice actually confessed to me that she really didn't think stuff like this could happen to her. She said she wouldn't have believed this feeling of true love was possible unless she experienced it first hand. Even though I tried to explain it to her as best I could, but it didn't seem realistic to her. Now she understands. She's totally in love with Evan and they're so excited to spend the rest of their lives together! Evan actually makes her heart skip a beat! She used to humor me when I'd tell her true love was out there, but now she sounds exactly like me! She said to me, "If you believe it's going to happen, it will happen. Something definitely has been guiding me through. If it wasn't for the confirmation I received by having three different people recommend that I meet Evan, I might not have gone on our second date, and I'm so glad I did!" It's amazing, isn't it? Timing is everything!

The beautiful thing about Janice's story is that she didn't let her bad experiences shape her outlook on life. It's very easy for people to become bitter after a divorce and close themselves off to new opportunities and relationships. People get easily discouraged, and understandably so. It's important to step back and look at the situation. Remember the story about my son spilling the milk? If your marriage doesn't work out, you can't go back and change things. You have to do your best to clean up the mess and move on. So you made a mistake! Learn from your experience, but don't let it define your life. Janice was able to look at her past relationships and realize why they didn't work. Then when she met Evan, she knew that the feelings she had for him were so different than what she had felt for men before. Learn from everything; even unpleasant experiences can be valuable!

In order to achieve bliss you have to acknowledge it. This means more than simply believing it exists; it means you have to follow your heart when you find it! I was speaking about relationships today to a dear friend of mine and she mentioned that she was attracted to someone but she couldn't understand where the attraction came from. "He's not nearly the 'type' of person I'm usually interested in. There are so many things about him that are different from what I usually look for. His personality, looks, behavior, etc." Despite all this, she said the attraction is so strong that she would really like to have the chance to get to know him better. Often times we let our head rule our hearts and that definitely gets in the way of finding love. Many people create some type of artificial standard in their mind, and have a list of criteria that someone has to meet to be worthy of their affection. Why limit yourself like that? Isn't it hard enough to find someone to share your life with? Why rule out people before you get to know them? Love isn't a laundry list of attributes you find pleasant. Love is an intangible element that takes your heart by storm.

I just wish people who plan to marry would make the decision with their heart, not with their head. Love is a feeling, an emotion. It's not logical, and it's certainly not a formula. If love could be summed up with a list of qualities that are desirable, then everyone would be happily married and there'd be no divorce. It just doesn't work that way. So many people look at their relationships and say, "Oh, he's so nice, he's good looking, he's got a great job, he'll make a great father and a great provider." That alone, to me, is the kiss of death! What happened to "He makes my heart stop when he walks through that door," or "She is what puts pep in my step every morning"? What about those feelings? You know, those feelings of the heart, the ones that make for wonderful fairy tale romances!

If I had sat down and made a bunch of rules about what type of person I wanted to marry, I probably wouldn't be with my husband today. He is far from perfect by definition, but he is perfect for me. There is nothing I would change about my husband. The best advice my father ever gave me was, if you are going to marry someone one day, make sure you can say to yourself, "There is nothing I would want to change about that person."

So, how is one to know when they've met Miss or Mr. Right? I think it's just a matter of being honest with yourself. If things don't feel completely right, don't try and convince yourself it's O.K. Always do what feels right in your heart, it's the answer to true happiness. You have to follow your heart . . . always.

***

The other day my seven year old asked me, "Why did you marry Daddy if you don't like him?"

I was dumbfounded! I replied, "What do you mean I don't like Daddy? I love Daddy!" Well, that day, I was expressing an opinion that my husband did not particularly agree with. TJ overheard our disagreement and his interpretation was that we did not love each other. I had to explain to my son that just because two people have a disagreement doesn't mean they don't love each other. In fact, a key component of a successful relationship is respecting each other's point of view, though it may be very different from your own. It's not about being right or wrong, it's about having a difference of opinion. We're not here to force our perspectives on others; we're here to share them, because when you share your opinion with others, you just might enlighten their world. On the other hand, you just might not! Whatever the case, you are entitled to your own opinion.

I taught my son, right then and there, that even though you don't agree with someone, it doesn't mean you don't love them. Kids hear arguments and they assume the worst. You need to let them know that people aren't always going to agree, and that's alright. It's so important to teach children at a very young age that even though there are times when you get upset with them, it doesn't change how much you love them.

My husband and I might not always agree, but we respect the fact that we each have our own beliefs and ideas. I love that my husband feels comfortable enough with me to voice his opinions freely. That type of communication is a key element in any marriage.

I didn't realize, until now, how incredibly vital trust is in a relationship. Without trust, you can't give fully of yourself. Without trust, there is fear of being rejected or judged. It's so wonderful to know that someone is totally honest with you and doesn't withhold anything in fear of hurting your feelings or even in fear of disagreement. Trust is the cornerstone in any solid relationship, whether it be your spouse, your sibling, your parents, or your friends. My husband and I share this kind of trust and respect, and it's what makes our marriage so successful. I know that I can count on my husband for anything, and he will always be there for me.

I'll never forget the support I received from my husband during the surgery I had to remove my tumor, although I wasn't aware of it at the time. All I remember is saying to the doctor, "Break a leg!" and off I went under general anesthesia. The next thing I knew, I was coming out of anesthesia in the recovery room and could barely focus on the very tall, handsome man by my side, my husband, Fred. He seemed like he was looking down at a ghost. I must have been one sight for sore eyes.

Later, the orderly in the hospital came up to me and said, "This man must really love you. I've been here over eight hours and he hasn't left your side once . . . not even to go to the bathroom or get something to eat. He hasn't even sat down this whole time." That's Fred for you, selfless. He actually could feel my pain and just knew not to leave my side. He was so scared that he was going to lose me. It's not every day your wife has a malignant tumor and part of her kidney removed. He stood there for hours praying and hoping that I was going to be O.K. Just the other night at dinner, nearly four years after my surgery, he mentioned how he was so scared by the idea that he almost lost me. It's something he'll never forget and it serves as a constant reminder for him about how important it is to cherish every moment you have. Fred knows that each day he spends with me is truly a gift. I wish everyone lived that way! I am so grateful to have a husband who is so thoughtful and caring.

Just the other day, I was in the living room singing karaoke and serenading my husband. I sang him the song "How Do I Live Without You" By Leann Rimes. If you've never heard the song, here are some of the lyrics:

> Without you, there'd be no sun in my sky
> There would be no love in my life
> There'd be no world left for me
> And I, oh baby, I don't know what I would do
> I'd be lost if I lost you

This song was to tell him, at that very moment, that he is "my everything." I didn't want to let a moment go by without letting him know how much he meant to me. After my cancer diagnosis, I realized I have to express these feelings while I can, and this seemed like a perfect moment to share my love. His eyes welled up with tears and he left the room, saying, "I can't listen to this." I knew that what he really meant was, "I am so scared to lose you because I really don't know how I will live without you." My intention was only to show him my love, but the power of the lyrics brought tears to his eyes. The moment was so emotional that it made him think about what life would be like without me. Our lives are one and the same. Whenever we are home, Fred enjoys having me underfoot. He always wants me right there, talking to him about our dreams, our fears and our next steps. If, God forbid, anything ever happened to me, who would be there to listen? Who would be there to dream with him and comfort him? I understood why he left the room.

Love can make us hurt, but at the same time, love is what pulls us through our most difficult times. My husband's father recently died, and it was, of course, devastating for all of us. Fred loved his father deeply, and losing him was incredibly painful. My father-in-law, or Poppy, as we liked to call him, was a World War II hero and had survived so much. He had been offered a full football scholarship to one of the best Ivy League schools in the nation, but passed on that incredible opportunity in order to enlist in the army and fight for his country. He was at the Battle of Iwo Jima, and received two separate battle wounds during the war. Poppy was honored with two purple hearts for his valor and courage.

He experienced his first heart attack when he was in his early forties and he went through several heart and bypass surgeries, as well as surgical procedures for his back and five aneurisms. In his wallet, he carried a list of medicines he was taking and medical procedures he had undergone. It was pages long! My father-in-law was a sickly man for nearly forty years and lived life on all different kinds of medications. When I say "lived life", he really did. He NEVER complained. He was a successful businessman and a loving family man as well as a highly respected and considerate friend to all he knew. He was one of the sweetest men I have ever met.

When my father-in-law became so sick that we needed to call in hospice care, none of us could accept that the end was near. Time and time again, Poppy pulled the rabbit out of his hat. He always fought his way to health and succeeded, but it was time to come to terms with the fact that he was no longer going to be part of our lives in the physical sense. He died a very peaceful death, at age seventy-nine, in his home with his family all around him.

When he passed away, Colonel Schwartz in Washington, D.C. called down to the local Marine barracks and ordered a funeral of the highest honor. Several Marines attended the funeral and Pops received a twenty-one gun salute at his burial site. It was a spectacular honor.

Shortly after his dad passed, Fred came home from driving his mom back to her now empty apartment in Garden City. He walked into the house and began to cry, and in his sadness, he managed to say, "I'm being very selfish because my father is up in heaven and is no longer suffering in pain. I'll just miss him, he was my best buddy."

I said to him, "You have to let yourself feel the way you feel. Regardless of how right it was for him to go at this time, it's still painful for those who loved him. You were so blessed to have him as long as you did. Your sadness comes from your loss, but you know your father is in a better place." While this was a very hard time for him, Fred knew that he would get through it because he had faith that his father was happy now and free from pain, and because he loved his father so much, he knew this was for the best. His memories of the happy times with his father got him through the pain and sadness of death. Love hurts, but love also heals.

Here's a letter Fred wrote to his dad as a tribute to him, which he read on the last night of his father's wake. I think it is an excellent example of how the fond memories of a loved one carry us through our grief:

Dear Dad,

Words cannot express the man you were, the father you were to Mary, Theresa and I, and the husband you were to Mom. You made us as proud of you as you were of us. All these years you showed us how to really love life and embrace it through good times and bad. Your whole presence and being is what has guided us, and through your teachings, you have shown us what family is all about. We continue to live your example through our own families today.

We stand before you today, Dad, knowing that through our prayers you will always hear us. To meet you was to love you. You embraced everyone and treated all with equal respect. Mom was the light of your life and she gave you so much joy and always kept your life full of fun. Mom also kept your life full of adventure and excitement. You can rest assured we'll continue to take care of her the way you would have wanted us to.

You always were there for our family through your kind and caring ways. We enjoyed your presence at all sporting events and birthday parties for your grandchildren. Your family meant the world to you and you meant the world to us, as well. Your positive outlook and strength penetrated all our lives including all your siblings, grandchildren, nieces and nephews.

You were so well loved among your peers, business associates, family and friends. You served your country and your family with dignity and honor. You were a tremendous athlete and scholar, and for the love of your country, you forwent scholarships to serve your country straight out of high school. You survived the battle of Iwo Jima, and you were highly decorated, receiving a Presidential Citation from President Truman.

You received not one, but two purple hearts. And speaking of hearts, yours endured so much. Through all your hospital procedures you had the tremendous will to live. You always seemed to pull the rabbit out of the hat time and time again. You were a man of strength, and never gave up. Now God has blessed and embraced you, and you are among all your loved ones that have passed before you. We find comfort knowing that you will be watching over us and we will continue to enjoy our lives through your example.

We love you always.

Your loving son,

Fred, Jr.

To know him was to truly love him; my father-in-law, the man I called Dad for ten years, the man who made me feel like his very own daughter. Now, here is a man who touched so many lives, and we never really knew until after he passed away. Two months after his passing, people were still calling to express their condolences as they found out about his death. These kind thoughts from friends and relatives helped us to get through the sadness we felt at his loss. Knowing that he touched so many people, and was so well thought of, made us feel so proud to have had him in our lives.

I remember at his funeral reception, one of his friends of over forty years got up to speak and mentioned that he had a story to describe the type of man Fred Ferrari was.

"When I was out of work with five children and no insurance coverage, Fred put me on his payroll so that my children would receive medical coverage until I was able to find another job," he said. "Fred didn't think twice about it. That is how giving he was. Fred Ferrari was a selfless man. He helped support many families including his own. When his car would need fixing, he would bring it to the same mechanic down the street every time, even though he knew the prices were a bit high. Fred knew that his mechanic had a family of his own to support, and so he never had a problem paying above and beyond normal charges. He knew that the money he was so fortunate to have was going to a good cause . . . the wife and children of this very hard working mechanic. Fred appreciated hard work and felt that this was his way of giving back. Regardless of whether there was a cheaper mechanic down the road, that didn't matter. What mattered to Fred was he was contributing to the man's livelihood."

What was so wonderful about Poppy's giving was that he made people feel so comfortable receiving from him. He never made it seem like charity, or a loan. He really did everything out of the goodness of his heart. I still can't believe I am blessed enough to have married his only son, and believe me, the apple does not fall far from the tree!

4

Death:
Live for the moment, for the moment is all we have.

DEATH IS A PART of life. Every day, babies are born and people die. It's part of the reality of our world, and something we can't escape. It's not a pleasant thought, and the loss of a loved one is never easy to deal with. Sometimes losing a person you love can feel like the end of the world. Coping with the passing of my father-in-law was very painful for my husband and I, but we got through it. The world didn't end, and eventually things got easier, and we were able to laugh and smile again. Fred's father had been at EVERY family celebration, whether it was a wedding, New Year's Eve, the Fourth of July, a birthday party, barbecues, etc. At every toast, from now on, there will be a mention of Fred's dad so we can honor his memory and know that he is with us still, at all our happy events. He will always be a part of our lives, and rather than grieve over his loss forever, we will celebrate his life.

One of the greatest gifts you can give someone is a fond memory. Be good to others while you can. If you care about someone, tell them now, while you have the chance. You never know where life may take you, or if you will have the opportunity in the future. Think about the people you've loved who have passed on, and all the happy memories you have of them. Aren't you thankful for those moments? Don't you want to leave your loved ones with memories like that?

It's amazing how our hearts, like our minds, have the capacity to hold so much! A childhood friend of mine, Gina, who I lost to leukemia, still holds a special place in my heart to this day. I had just entered the seventh grade, and it was a time when all the local elementary schools from different towns came together to attend one junior high. Gina had attended Locust Valley Elementary school and I attended the Bayville Elementary School, but now life had brought us together at Locust Valley Junior High. I met Gina in art class where we became good friends. She was a somewhat quiet girl who was very bright; she was in all honors classes and enjoyed school. We used to sit next to each other in class and she enjoyed me because I was a bit of her lighter side and I enjoyed her because she was a bit of my more serious, academic side.

Gina was always getting sick and it worried me terribly. It seemed like there was always something wrong. Once she had this horrible cough and I asked her what was wrong. She told me the doctor said she had bronchitis. Well, one day, I remember like it was yesterday, Gina didn't come to school. I didn't think much of it at first, since she was sick pretty often, but her chair stayed empty, for a long, long time.

Gina was diagnosed with a very advanced stage of leukemia. I don't recall the specifics of her illness, because I was so young at the time, but I do remember her losing all her hair. She went through intense chemotherapy at Sloane Kettering Memorial Cancer Hospital in Manhattan. They did everything possible to keep her alive, but I guess God had a reason for taking her early, even if we may never understand that reason.

Gina died shortly after she was diagnosed with this life threatening illness. I couldn't bring myself to go to Gina's funeral. It was too painful and I could not understand how someone so young could be taken from us. I was not even a teenager yet. After Gina died, it took a very long time for her friends to feel that there was any kind of normalcy to their days. Gina was an integral part of all her friend's lives and it wasn't easy to come to terms with this loss. Gina was only a child, and so were we. We had no experience with death or loss, and it was so difficult for us to conceive of this tragedy. Despite the sadness, Gina's memory will always be in the hearts of those who knew her. She was a beautiful soul who made a strong impression on us all. She was such a pleasure to be around. I can still remember her face, so many years later, as if she was standing right in front of me. It's funny, I can only remember her smiling.

***

When someone you love leaves this earth, it's amazing how it changes your life forever. You are full of sorrow and you can never really express to another person exactly how you feel, because it's so personal and so profound. There is no way to explain how deep the pain runs when you lose a loved one. You may feel estranged from people around you no matter how much you love them. Believe me, they will understand that you are going through a rough time. There is no right or wrong way to work through grief, and you should never feel guilty if you need some time alone or if it's taking you a while to recover. Some have the ability to put it aside a lot better than others. Everyone deals with death differently but the underlying common ground is that the pain will dissipate with time. It will get better eventually. It's incredible that through all pain and anguish, our hearts endure.

No one has ever died of a broken heart. The pain will subside, and life will go on. Your life may never be the same, but you can be happy again. It's about hope. Fill your mind with nurturing thoughts not doomsday thoughts. It makes a difference. In fact, it makes all the difference in the world. Your perception is and always will be your reality. Does this mean we can will our lives in the direction we would like them to go? To some extent, yes. Did you ever notice people who are hopeful are happier than people who are not? That's because without hope, things seem to go awry. Have you noticed that your more negative, less hopeful friends are not as happy as those that are more optimistic? If you look past the clouds, and look for that sunshine, you will find it.

You have to make a conscious effort to enjoy life each day. One of the greatest gifts we have is life and the ability to enjoy it. I try to appreciate every breath I take, and be grateful for every moment I have on this earth. I believe that the best way to deal with death is to appreciate our own lives. No one should die in vain. When you lose a loved one, don't spend the rest of your life in miserable solitude, that's not what they would have wanted! Let the experience open your eyes and make you realize that your life is precious and you should live it to the fullest. Of course, it takes time, and everyone has to move at their own pace, but it's important to always remember that things will get better. You still have your life, so appreciate it!

Death is so final. For those of us who are left here on earth, it can seem like a difficult task to continue and prevail with all the pain and suffering we experience throughout our living years. If you think about it, we endure sickness, death, tragedy, and watch our loved ones endure it as well. Sometimes it feels unbearable, but then something inside you helps you to keep trudging forward in hopes for a better tomorrow.

I have a good friend who lost her husband and she told me that she felt she had not yet learned to move on with her life, even though she had seen other friends go through this and move forward. She couldn't relate to the idea of moving on, or imagine herself ever doing so. She just wasn't ready yet. She will be one day, that's a guarantee. However, I guess it's like watching all your friends get married when you don't even have a boyfriend; you could never imagine yourself as a bride until you've met the right person to share your life with. When you lose someone, it often feels like you will never be able to move on, because you simply can't imagine yourself getting past the pain. Until you're finally ready to accept what has happened, you can't see the light at the end of the tunnel. Even if you don't see the light, you have to keep telling yourself that it exists. You may not feel ready to move on, but you need to look at those around you and see that they have all endured death and loss, and their lives have gone on. Everyone deals with death eventually. It is inevitable. Yet all these people who have lost someone continue to be happy and have relationships and love again. The world doesn't stop turning. It only feels that way.

***

My friend Grace was four months pregnant with her second son, Joey, when her husband, John, suddenly became ill with a very rare blood disease. His respiratory system soon failed and he died fourteen days after he was admitted into the hospital. Prior to this, her husband was the picture of health. He owned a gym that offered personal training services, and it was more than just a business. Exercise was something he was very involved in; his muscles had muscles. He was always health conscious about everything he ate. It was one of those sudden, unexpected tragedies. Grace was a devoted wife and mother when her husband passed away. John and Grace were high school sweethearts and they absolutely adored each other. When John died, Grace became incredibly introverted. She conversed with no one outside her close family and friends and dreaded the idea of even looking in another man's eyes. She had lost the love of her life.

Grace was barely thirty years old at the time and practically newly married. Her mother moved in with her to help with the kids, and make things easier for Grace. It just so happened that her husband John was approved for an increase in his life insurance policy about a month prior to him passing. It was just in time. Financially, Grace was left in an O.K. situation where she was able to live on the money from the insurance policy, but emotionally, she was a wreck. Grace had lost her father about a year prior to John passing away. She had a very close relationship with her father, and losing the two most significant men in her life within one year was devastating for her. Thankfully, her mother was there to help her through the most difficult time in her life, and she stuck by Grace's side through all her emotional ups and downs.

Grace and I had met a year before her husband passed, but we became very close when her older son, Johnny, was three and Joey was one. My sons happened to be the exact same age as Johnny and Joey. Interestingly, Grace's husband and my husband knew each other in high school and we happened to both move to the same town, on the same block. I like to think that the friendship of my sons and I helped Grace through most of her difficult times. I feel as if we met each other for a reason. We became friends at this difficult time in her life, and we had all these interesting connections; it's as if we were meant to meet so that I could be there for her in her time of need.

Well, one day, a friend of Grace's insisted that Grace meet her friend Matthew. Grace immediately fell head over heels for Matthew. Here was a woman who was ill over the thought of dating another man, and yet, within one date, she fell in love.

Grace couldn't believe that she was capable of loving another man. We talked for hours and hours about how guilty she felt, as if she was committing adultery. Even though she was in love with Matthew, she was having a very hard time getting past the death of her husband. She was terrified of loving someone else, and she felt as if she were betraying her husband by loving another man. But Matthew understood. Matthew is a wonderful, caring man who is full of faith. He honestly felt that John had sent him to Grace for a reason. He believed their love was meant to be, that he was there to help Grace heal.

Eventually, Grace was able to overcome her feelings of guilt and see that life has to go on. She knew her husband would want her to be happy, and that he would approve of Matthew. At her wedding, I cried as if I was at a funeral, my tears were like Niagara Falls! I knew how much she had been through for the past several years, and to be able to see her in total bliss was absolutely marvelous. It was so emotional and so wonderful. As she walked down the aisle with her son Johnny, he asked her, "Why is Mrs. Ferrari crying?" Now how do you explain that one to a seven year old?!

Grace and Matthew just had a son together, and they're so happy. There are moments when she still feels guilty that she is here enjoying her life and John never had the opportunity to see his sons grow up, but she knows that instead of feeling guilty, she should be thankful for the time she had with John, and the beautiful children he gave her. Both Johnny and Joey love Matthew like a father and he has embraced them as his sons in such a natural way. It's astounding how a story that started so tragically has such a fairy tale ending. Some things are just meant to be!

***

Not too long ago, I called a friend of mine who hadn't shown up for a lunch we had planned. When she answered the phone, her voice was hysterical with disbelief and she kept crying the words, "My father's dying . . . my father's dying!" and then she just hung up. I felt numb. I wanted to help her, but what could I do?

About twenty minutes later he passed away. Her father had suffered for two years from colon cancer that metastasized to the liver and, soon after, to the lungs and stomach. He was what one would call a "gentle giant." He was a sweet and wonderful man, and he was so healthy and full of life prior to being diagnosed with cancer. He fought his battle for more than two years and his body just couldn't fight any longer.

At the funeral, the priest mentioned that we really don't know when we will leave this earth, but one thing is for sure, we were born to die. He said death has no bias. Age, gender, creed, health, these things don't matter. He reminded us that, despite all this, love will never die. The love and the memories that we hold in our hearts will last forever. All the faith in the world will not bring back the long chats, the laughs, the stories . . . and boy, could he tell a story . . . or two . . . or three. All the faith in the world will not bring back his warm being, his guiding ways, or his loving touch. But our faith lets us know that he is in a better place now, and that does so much to alleviate the pain. Through our faith, we know that he can now rest peacefully, and that serves as a great comfort to all who loved him.

I had a few words with the grandson of my friend's father who had just passed away. He was very torn up over the death of his Grandpa. We were talking about how his Grandpa will watch over him for the rest of his life, and that he is in a better place where he is at peace. I hope he found comfort in my words.

I know that if my cancer were to take a turn for the worse, those close to me will find comfort in knowing that I am in a better place. They know that although I will no longer be on this earth with them, I will be in a wonderful place. I'm not denying the incredible sadness my loved ones will feel when I am gone, and no longer with them physically, but I will definitely be with them in spirit! They will find comfort in knowing that I will always be watching over them.

***

When I first took a cruise to the Bahamas, I didn't realize that the boat was part of the vacation. I viewed the ship as just a means of transportation. We can't view life as just a means of transportation to heaven, we must enjoy the ride. It's easier said than done. How do we enjoy the ride when there is tragedy, death and sickness all around us? How do we enjoy the ride when there are people who struggle just to get out of bed in the morning? How do we enjoy life when there are so many people walking this earth in misery? We have to stay positive and be thankful for every breath we take. We should look at our own good fortune and be grateful, and try to do the best we can to help others. Look to your right and look to your left to lend a helping hand. If you're blessed enough to have the means to help someone else, then you absolutely should.

When you help others, you realize that things really aren't so hopeless. Life can seem rough at times, when you think about how much tragedy there is in the world. But when you do your part to help those who are less fortunate, then you're helping to make the world a better place for everyone. Now you have a purpose, a reason to keep moving forward, and you can see the bigger picture.

Have purpose and joy and love in your life. Make your moments count. When we lose someone and there's no bringing them back, you go into the "I wish" stage. "I wish I got to tell him how much I really love him despite our differences," or "I wish I didn't let that argument get in the way of our relationship." We must enjoy our moments and not get caught up in all the petty things that keep us from enjoying life to its fullest. When I catch myself arguing with my children, sometimes I do stop and think, and say to myself, I really need to pick my battles. Why fight over something silly? What if you never get the chance to apologize? Imagine how that would feel next time you argue with someone you love. If we would all take a moment to stop and breathe and think about what's really important, we could certainly avoid a lot of arguments and aggravation. We could avoid all those regrets, too.

***

Last Thanksgiving, we spent the holiday with my in-laws. I love Fred's family dearly, and I had a wonderful time, but the day was saddened by the absence of a dear family member. My brother-in-law Ronnie recently lost his father, Hank. Hank had passed away very suddenly around Halloween, and now we were all joined together as a family without his wonderful presence.

It just wasn't the same without him. Hank was a man who really knew how to enjoy life. He was seventy-seven years old; he would have been seventy-eight on December 6th. Thanksgiving was a painful day for the family. His son Ronnie said grace before dinner, but he could barely get out the words "Happy Thanksgiving." It was far from happy.

Hank's death was difficult for everyone. On the day he died, Ronnie's best friend Don happened to have car trouble, and pulled into Hank's driveway just as Hank's wife Genevieve came running out for help. Hank had just lost consciousness and Don did his best to revive Hank, but it was too late. Everyone took it very hard.

The funeral mass was so heartfelt. All of Hank's grandchildren got up to speak, and they came up with a top ten list of what they will miss most about Grandpa. The number one thing they will miss about

Grandpa is the money he would give them for their report cards! It gave everyone a nice laugh, which was sorely needed. Next, Ronnie got up and spoke. I'm sure it must have been incredibly difficult for Ronnie to stand up and speak about his father when he was undergoing so much pain and emotional suffering! Yet he spoke about his father in such a lovely way, it was a beautiful moment. Despite his pain, he wanted to share his thoughts about a man he loved so much. He did it, and he did it well.

This may sound so strange, but I thought to myself that Hank would have loved to have attended his own funeral. He was a man full of knowledge and history, a strong, proud military veteran. He was buried at Calverton, a national military cemetery. They played taps and two soldiers folded the flag and handed it to Hank's wife Genevieve. The soldier who presented Genevieve with his veteran flag said, "On behalf of the United States of America, we present to you this flag." It was such a patriotic moment! Hank would have been so proud.

The next morning, after the funeral, my husband asked me if I could run down to the basement to find something for him. As I was looking around, I noticed a plastic box sitting on the very top of a bin full of junk. I looked at it wondering what it was, and decided to open it. The box was full of tapes dating back almost four years, and I hadn't looked at them since then.

Well, it was the very box of tapes Hank brought us for our annual 4th of July four years ago! These tapes were made by Hank himself, and they took him months to mix from his old LPs. He labeled each and every tape; we must have over forty of them! These tapes were a collaboration of the big bands, Glen Miller, Frank Sinatra, etc. They were full of musical history and I was so grateful for them, because I love and appreciate all types of music, and I especially appreciated the thought that Hank had put into them. It was just so amazing that the first thing I picked up happened to be from Hank.

Things like this happen to us all the time and they are clearly not coincidences! They are much more than that. Each and every one of us experience coincidences that go far beyond any logical explanation. It's all about accepting, without another thought, that things do happen in our lives that are small blessings. Things happen for a reason, and I knew that it was no coincidence that I found these precious memories of Hank that would help carry on his legacy after his death.

I was so thankful to have this reminder of Hank, and I wanted so much to share this story with his family but I knew that at this time, it would be hard for them to see past their pain. It's always hard to express your condolences, especially when whatever you say or do doesn't seem to help. What could I say to Hank's immediate family? How do you extend yourself in this time of grief? Only time can heal their wounds, but knowing how much Hank was loved could bring them some sense of peace. I knew I couldn't heal their pain, but I wanted to do what I could to let them know that Hank's life was a wonderful and meaningful one. I wanted to write them a letter to share my beautiful memories of Hank.

***

It Was Truly a Pleasure

To the Furman Family,

Thank you for sharing Hank with us all these years! For a man who had such a love for music, his life was truly underplayed. I can remember speaking to Hank about music and how much he enjoyed the big bands; Glen Miller, Frank Sinatra, Barbara Streisand, etc. I told him that one of my dreams was to have that music piped into every room in the house, playing all day long!

It was three years ago at our 4th of July party out east. While everyone else brought wine and desserts, Hank brought boxes of tapes for us to enjoy. I was so appreciative that Hank had spent months mixing these tapes for our enjoyment. I look forward to one day having his tapes playing throughout our house.

Hank was a man who brightened the room with his presence. He was tremendously knowledgeable, yet not at all pretentious. He had a way of explaining anything to anyone, even his grandchildren. Every year, he would give the kids wonderful presents, rare coins or just rare anything, things you never even knew existed. Hank watched them open the presents with such enjoyment. They were actually presents to remember him by, not just another doll or another toy that had a short life span, but a memory his grandchildren will cherish for the rest of their lives.

It was apparent that his thoughtfulness was second nature to Hank, especially with his family. He appeared to receive enjoyment in life just by observing the happiness of his family. He was the glue that held the family together, the compass that directed the family through life. He seemed to always be enjoying life; he was never upset or angry, just extremely content with his life and his family.

In closing, we will miss Hank's presence, his warmth, his strong handshakes and his bear hugs! When we said goodbye to all of you the night of the funeral, Bitty, my Goddaughter, came up to me to say goodbye and gave me the biggest squeeze. It was the type of hug that compresses the lungs and takes your breath away. I said to her, "I only know one other person who gives great hugs like that." She asked "Who?" and I said "Your Grandpa!"

We find comfort in knowing that Hank is home now in a better place with all the big band greats!

With love,

Susan

***

I believe it's so important to lend a comforting thought to people in their time of need. Kind words aren't going to take away all the pain of death, but imagine if someone close to you died, and no one offered their condolences. Imagine if no one had anything nice to say about the loved one you lost. How horrible! It is reassuring for people to know that those who died did not die in vain. They want to know that their loved ones were respected and cared for, and that they touched the lives of others. By letting Hank's family know that Hank was an important part of our lives, and that we will always remember him, we helped them to know that his memory and legacy will always live on.

A couple of months after Hank's funeral, on what would have been his seventy-eighth birthday, I attended a charity function near my home. Hank's wife Genevieve happened to be there, since her son thought it would be a good idea to take her out. He wanted her to have a nice day and enjoy life instead of sitting at home by herself. He knew what a difficult day it would be for her. She's lucky to have such a wonderful, supportive family, and to cap it all off,

Genevieve won a beautiful painting in a raffle that day. It was like she was getting a special gift on a day when she normally would have been giving gifts. It was almost as if Hank was watching over her, trying to cheer her up!

***

Death isn't the only hardship we deal with in life. We come across all types of situations which make life more difficult. It could be death, sickness, divorce, or even things as simple as having a bad day at work, or fighting with your spouse. We are allowed to be frustrated, or sad, or angry about the adversity and troubles we face every day. The key is not letting those negative feelings get the best of you. It's only natural to be angry or sad sometimes, but you don't want those feelings to linger too long. You want to be able to look around you and say, "Hey, today wasn't the best day, but that doesn't mean tomorrow can't be great." Some people want to wallow in their misery, and feel sorry for themselves. What kind of life is that?

My hope is that by sharing these stories, I can show people that even immense tragedy can be overcome. I know people who have been through so much, but they have persevered and lived happy lives, and their stories are so inspiring. Whenever I'm feeling down, I think about what some of my friends have been through, and I know if they can get through such hardship, I can certainly get past my troubles.

Through all our life experiences, even the difficult ones, we are constantly learning. Learning helps us to achieve happiness. Happiness is a constant struggle in a world filled with tragedies, sickness, and death. However, if we look for the beauty and the joy in all of our days, it seems to make the struggle that much easier. Life is a blessing that you will only truly know if you let yourself live.

I'd like to close with a toast that my husband wrote to his father after the funeral. Fred's dad was known as "the toastmaster" to all that knew him. When he spoke, no one followed because they never could hold a candle to his words. Fred did his best to capture the spirit of his father, and I believe this toast is a beautiful example of remembering the positive things about his father who passed, rather than dwelling in the grief of his passing.

***

A Toast to Dad

Dad, you were always the man I hoped one day to be
Full of faith, love and kindness for my children to see
This toast I give before you will be said in rhyme, too
As "toastmaster", that's one thing you never thought to do
As a father you were the very best for me
And as you would say, you were "the man you dared to be"
You served your country, two purple hearts you did receive
Your life was so accomplished, hard for most to conceive
You were a scholar, an athlete, and fought for us all
It is now I stand before you, so very proud and tall
It is you who made me the man I am today

BLESSED BEYOND WORDS

And I will continue to live your legend, each and every day
You traveled the world, Naples, Venice, the Amalfi shore
You had it all, and enjoyed life so much more
When you went to Rome, they would say you looked like the Pope
It is from within you that we found faith, love, and hope
Dad, you were the finest in all that you did
When my shoes weren't polished, it was from you that I hid
You taught me to be punctual and showed me the way
So that I could make a nice life for my family one day
I, as well, have accomplished so much in so little time
It is because of your teachings that I am doing so fine
You taught me to keep knocking on those doors that said "no"
Because one day, you said, "they're bound to order, you just never know."
We always seemed to have a full barbecue by the pool
And I remember the Yankee games when you kept me home from school
We laughed and yelled and we seemed to have it all
We loved to watch every sport together, especially baseball
You are so well loved by many people as well as groups still
You're the only man listed in the cookbook for Mom's Club of Flower Hill
No other author could come close to write the book on sales & life
You took me page by page and I will continue to write
For my children one day will look back and say "wow"
It was my dad and my poppy for whom they'll be so proud
How one man accomplished so much in just seventy-nine years

Is amazing to us all and now brings us to tears

I will miss you so much, I've known you since birth

You will now look over all of us while we remain here on earth

In closing, dear father, there's one more thing I must say
God Bless you, Semper Fidelis, and as your son
I salute you today!

***

Though we hear and see and deal with pain and suffering all around us, there is still opportunity for happiness. We need to acknowledge that death is a reality, which most people cannot foresee. It's about coming to terms with the reality that sickness and suffering is part of life and that if we ourselves are struck with it, we will learn to endure it. There are so many beautiful things in life to appreciate and to enjoy. Sometimes we just need to find them; they're right there, all around us. If you look up for a moment you could probably list a page worth of blessings around you: a baby, a loving mother, siblings getting along (rare, but seek and you shall find), the creation of man made things that help us to better live our lives each day, the comfort of being with someone we love, our homes, our children, our friends, our families...

5

Family:
Life without family is like ice cream without a cone.

THROUGH THE GOOD times and the bad, I know that I will always have my family. Our families are so important, and yet we often take them for granted. They've always just been there, and so we don't think about how amazing that really is. Who else is there for you through thick and thin? We are tied to our families through blood bonds, and those are not easy to break. There is nothing like family.

My sister Amy has been one of my greatest inspirations in life. Amy is a few years older than my twin and I, and around the time we were born, Amy was diagnosed with autism. She was about two and a half years old. Back then, they had very few schooling options for mentally handicapped children. In fact, they didn't know much about autism at all. I remember asking my parents what happened to Amy to make her the way she was. The answers varied from "Not enough oxygen at birth," to, "It's a mishap in her genes," to, "It's hereditary." Yet no one else in our family that we knew of had autism. No one really had an answer.

Growing up with an autistic sister became a very difficult situation socially. I don't mean that it made our social lives difficult; none of us were embarrassed or ashamed of Amy. Society just didn't understand, and people would behave rudely around us. I would often see adults tell their children to keep away, like Amy was some untamed animal. It made me so upset to see adults act in such a manner. How could they be so insensitive to a child? Time and time again, I saw both adults and children who were frightened by Amy's behavior. She would have tantrums at any given moment; she simply couldn't control it. I could understand children being scared because they don't know better, but adults? It saddened me. Yes, Amy was different. It didn't make her any less human or any less deserving of decent treatment. Yet people would stare and say things.

I remember once walking into a department store when I was very small, and my twin sister and I were each holding one of Amy's hands. People just stared. I remember staring back at one child and asking, "What are you looking at?" I wanted to explain to everyone in that store, and everyone in the world, that you don't have to be scared of people just because they're different. Everyone is an individual, and none of us are exactly the same. If we avoid people because they're different from us, we will never make friends or have meaningful relationships! It's so important to look beneath the surface and find out who someone really is inside. None of these strangers were interested in knowing how amazing Amy was, all they saw was a little girl who wasn't like them. They would stare at her without even thinking that they might be hurting her or those who love her.

Now when I'm in a public place and I see a mentally handicapped child with a parent, I start talking to them, letting them know that I have an autistic sister. I get such nice response from people. It's like there is a bond between us, because it's so hard to understand what it's like to live with a mentally handicapped child unless you've done it yourself. I know these people are constantly subjected to the kind of stares and whispers that Amy was, and I want to let them know that someone understands.

When I was younger, I used to sing with Amy. We've always shared a love of music. Amy is wonderfully talented when it comes to music, and from a very, very young age, she was able to remember the lyrics to every song she heard. She could play the piano without ever taking a lesson; she would just figure out what notes to play from listening to the music. One of her favorite songs was "There's a Place For Us" by Barbara Streisand. Even though Amy lived mostly in a world all her own, it was like that song told her that it was ok, that she was special for a reason. It always reminded me that there is a place in this world for Amy, even if it isn't Mainstream USA. Amy would sing every word, perfectly on key, telling me that she knew there was a place for her and she would be alright.

Having Amy in my life helped me realize that people are made differently, but that doesn't make them any less equal. Every life is precious, and everyone is special in their own unique way. Having Amy as my sister has really shaped me into the type of human being I've become; she taught me to be understanding to all people, regardless of race, nationality and abilities. We were all put here to take part in the world as best we can, and Amy has definitely touched the lives of many people. She has made the world a brighter place.

My mother recently told me that she always considered Amy a blessing, despite her illness. She told me that being around Amy helped make all her children more empathetic towards others, and I do see this trait in all my siblings. My mother told me a story of a boy named Joey who lived in our neighborhood when I was little. Joey had Down syndrome, and all the other children would steer clear of him. But she says my brothers and sisters were very compassionate toward Joey. She also mentioned how my brother Casey became a scout leader, and always made it a point to help others whenever he could. We all had a very different outlook on life than the other children, because we lived with Amy and knew not to be scared of people's differences.

Not only has Amy enriched the lives of her siblings, but she's also touched the lives of her nephews and nieces, as well. I can definitely see Amy's influence on my own children. At a very early age, my sons would keep somewhat of a distance from Amy. They didn't quite understand why Aunt Amy behaved differently than the rest of us. As they got a little older, I explained to them that God doesn't make everyone the same, and Aunt Amy is just different, but different doesn't mean wrong. I let them know that Aunt Amy is very special and has her own unique talents and abilities, just as they have theirs. Now that they are older, they have learned how to relate to and communicate with their aunt. It's really incredible to see the empathy my children show toward their aunt as well as toward other children that face handicaps, both physical and emotional. When they spend time with their aunt, and see how loving and amazing she is, they realize that people can be incredibly wonderful on the inside, despite how they may appear. They've learned to look past people's differences and to get to know them for who they really are.

Autistic people truly live in a world of their own, a world without judgment. Amy has the innocence of a small child, and she's simply incapable of being skeptical. The lessons I've learned from her are invaluable. I look at her and I see what the world could be like if people were kinder and less negative. Amy never judges others or assumes things, it's like she was brought into the world to show us a better way to be.

This past Memorial Day, I invited my family to a barbeque at our summer home in Westhampton. We relaxed by the pool, shared a good meal, and just enjoyed each other's company. Well, Memorial Day happened to be Amy's birthday, so I told Amy I would take her shopping wherever she wanted so she could pick out something for her special day. The town of Westhampton Beach in New York is full of upscale shops and boutiques. There is beautiful clothing, shoes, make-up, simply incredible items all over the place. So I asked Amy which store she wanted to go in. She said, "Rite Aid."

"Rite Aid, Amy? Are you sure?" I asked.

She replied, "Yes, Rite Aid. I want to get my instant camera pictures developed and I want lots of magazines and more instant cameras to take pictures so that I can put them into my photo album that is in my group home."

Happy to please my sister on her birthday, I replied, "Well, Amy, that sounds like a plan!" Off we went to Rite Aid. Now, what I didn't know was that my mother had taken Amy the day before to get magazines . . . eleven magazines. On Amy's birthday, she picked out ten more magazines with me. Amy loves fashion magazines and magazines with lots of people in them; she loves to look at pictures. We then purchased a couple of instant cameras and went up to the one hour photo lab to drop off Amy's film. She was so excited that it would be done in one hour!

I asked Amy where else would she like to go shopping for her birthday while we waited for her pictures to be developed, and she said, "Susan, I would like to go back to the car and sit and read my magazines and pick up my photographs when they're ready."

"Is that all you would like, Amy?" I asked.

Amy just took both her hands and clapped them together in such glee with a hearty laugh and said, "Yes!"

When we think about material possessions and things we buy each other for birthday celebrations, we always want more! Amy has simple pleasures in life. She loves magazines and taking pictures and of course, listening to music. She appreciates these small things, and is thankful for what she's given. Seeing that Amy really doesn't understand limitations, I thought she was going to take me to the cleaners when I told her I was going to treat her to a day of shopping in Westhampton. Well, it took all of ten minutes to make Amy satisfied and happy as a clam! It was a joy to see Amy so ecstatic with her photos and magazines. We could all learn from her what a better place the world would be without so much commercialism. Amy understands that life is all about the little things!

**

Amy's autism affected my family in a purely positive way. Unfortunately, most people who have never had an autistic family member aren't able to see the positive side of raising an autistic child. Many people have selfish instincts, and can only think about the time, stress and money involved in raising a mentally handicapped child. I have to admit, it is a strenuous burden at times, but that's just the way it is and we wouldn't have changed it for anything in the world. Amy is a blessing.

Amy has had incredible achievements despite her autism. Really, I don't think of it as a handicap at all. It doesn't hold her back or keep her from doing anything, she just views the world in a different way. Every year she appears in a musical for The Free Players of Long Island, using all of her musical talents. She participated in the Baton Rouge, Louisiana Special Olympics, and won a gold medal in both the 200 yard dash and the gymnastics competition.

Amy was among the twenty athletes who were selected from the United States to represent the Special Olympics in Holland. I remember Nike suited her up to perform. She got to meet Princess Marguerite and Prince Wilhelm, and Amy was just plain old Amy. She asked Prince Wilhelm if he enjoyed the glockenspiel, and amazingly, the prince replied that it was his favorite instrument! She had no qualms about asking the princess if she liked Donna Summer, too. They just chatted away like old pals. My mother was in shock. To her, it was like meeting the President of the United States, and she had been so nervous. She couldn't believe how Amy was so chatty and relaxed, but the prince really seemed to take a liking to Amy! My mother was so proud of Amy and all she had done at the Special Olympics. She said it was so wonderful to watch Amy, standing there on the podium, waiting to receive her medal. As people from all the participating nations marched for the Special Olympics ceremony, there was Amy, proudly representing the United States.

When my mother and Amy returned home from Holland after their ten day trip, my father went to pick them up at the airport. He couldn't believe it when he saw all these children with Down syndrome hugging my mother. My dad said, "You only spent ten days with them and look at how affectionate they are toward you."

My mom replied, "I've learned more about humanity from each of these children than anywhere else in the world. It was a marvelous experience for me because it just made it so much more apparent that each and every one of us has something to offer."

***

I have another sister, Eve-lynn, my twin. I like to call her my birth buddy. I am thankful for her every day and she is always in my prayers. Though we are on two totally different ends of the spectrum, we have this unbelievable underlying ability to understand each other. Maybe that's why I have such an ability to understand all types of people, because I was given a twin sister with whom I shared my life, who has basically nothing in common with me, except for our love for each other! We have no secrets between us and we are truly best friends. Sometimes it amazes me how we can be so close when we're so different. That's the beauty of family! We have that incredible sibling bond that brings us together.

I remember when we both went off to college, I struggled more with the separation of my twin sister then my high school sweetheart! I'll never forget, it was like someone tore my heart out. I missed her so much. We joke that our parents would have saved so much more money if they just sent us to the same school because each month our phone bill was like a mortgage payment! We would spend hours on the phone!

One evening, while we were both away at school, we were chatting about everything and nothing at all, as we always did. We're always so interested in hearing about each other's lives. I was telling Evelynn that I had this unexplainable, horrible pain in my arm. She said that was funny, because her arm was in a sling because she hurt it very badly. I said back to her, "Well, that explains it!" As crazy as it sounds, when you're a twin, you really do experience each other's pain and suffering as if it's your own. It's really the best way I can describe the kind of bond twins have. Once when we were children, we both woke up one morning crying that there was a gorilla in our closet. Our parents thought we were crazy, but we had both woken up from the same bad dream. Unless, of course, there really was a gorilla in our closet!

Twins really do have this unexplainable bond that no one can understand except another twin. I know it sounds crazy to all those non-twins out there. Even our own mother could never understand our relationship. We are fraternal twins and we are so different, yet we are extremely close. A family is made up of all different kinds of personalities and it is so important to respect everyone's differences and understand that we're not always going to agree or have the same choice in clothes, food, or all sorts of other things. Respecting each other's differences is what family is all about. Being so close to Eve-lynn, while at the same time being so different from her, taught me that you can have an incredible relationship with someone, even if you have nothing in common.

Growing up with Eve-lynn was like growing up with a best friend who was always there, 24/7. Being a twin is truly one of God's gifts; there is nothing like it. It's something people can't really understand unless they've experienced it. It goes beyond just being siblings, we are eternally linked. We are like two parts of a whole. The thought of life without my twin would be like a piece of me was missing. We've always stood by each other, throughout our childhood, and even as adults. We've been each other's cheerleaders through life, supporting each other through everything.

***

My brother Casey has two children; his youngest child is autistic and his name is Casey Matthew. I'll never forget the day he was born, he had a very difficult time and was in ICU for quite a while. We were not sure if he was going to make it. I remember the look on my brother's face was one of such fear, fear of losing his second child. Casey Matthew pulled through, though, and his birth was truly a blessing.

Casey Matthew was diagnosed with autism at the early age of two years old. He was a very happy baby and loved to be loved. He loved to be hugged and kissed and would pull your face to his little cheek for a kiss. When I first found out Casey Matthew was diagnosed with autism, I knew Casey and his family were going to have a difficult time with it. But as I watch my brother handle his son in such a loving manner, it reminds me of how Amy had the same effect on our family.

Casey is so enthralled with his son; I've never once heard him say, "I wish I had a son I could take to sporting events or throw a football around with." Casey absolutely loves sports. He had a football scholarship to a division III school and was captain of his team when they won the national championship. He was on television and received a national championship ring. Right after college, Casey opened up his own sporting goods store because he enjoyed keeping the sports enthusiasm going in the community. Now he was faced with fathering his only son, who was autistic. Casey would never have the opportunity to have his son follow in his footsteps. This all sounds so sad, but to Casey and Casey Matthew, life is good.

Casey enjoys helping his son in his every day rituals. Having Casey Matthew in his life has been incredibly enriching and has taught him so much. Casey has just completed his teacher's license in special education to help other children like his son.

***

Family is the nucleus of our lives. Life begins with family and ends with family. It is so important to have understanding, support, and most important, unconditional love in your family. It is your family that understands and is always forgiving when you sometimes do not make the best choices. Whether you are a mother, a spouse, a sibling, a daughter, or a son, you always find comfort in knowing that no matter how bad things get, you have your family to support you. On the other hand, when there are good things to share, your family is always there to be happy for you and share in your joy. It's so difficult to put into words how important family really is. The way I like to describe it is, life without family is like ice cream without a cone or a burger without a bun. Without family, you just couldn't enjoy life to its fullest. My son's favorite expression is, "A kiss without a hug is like ice cream without sprinkles!"

Of course, when I talk about family, I don't mean it has to be a family in the most traditional sense. Sometimes families aren't the complete units that we usually think of. Step-parents and in-laws aren't related by blood, but they're family. Sometimes, "family" can mean those friends that are so close to you that they feel like brothers and sisters. What's important is having people in your life that you can look to when you need a shoulder to cry on or a helping hand, the people who will always be there for you even when times are rough. That's family. It isn't always the people that are related to you by blood.

My friend Lisa has learned a lot about the real meaning of family. This was a woman that had it all; the husband, the family, the money, the lifestyle, everything. One day, out of the blue, her husband throws down a bunch of pictures on the table. He shows her the pictures and says, "I have another family and I'm leaving you." She thought he was kidding at first, that it was some kind of a sick joke or something. She couldn't believe that such a thing was really happening. Then he went into the backyard where their fifteen year old was swimming and said, "Bye honey, I'm leaving."

The child responded, "O.K. Daddy, I'll see you later."

Her father just looked at her and said, "No, I'm really leaving, and I'm never coming back." To this day, he has never returned nor has he spoken to his daughter again. That was about ten years ago.

Now, when Lisa first shared her story with me, I felt like I was listening to a movie plot, that's how unreal it sounded to me. How does a man, after thirty years of marriage, not only have an affair, but a complete other family, to boot?! Not only that, but how does he just sever the relationship in such a cold way? It was like a knife to the heart. How do things like this happen?!?

In retrospect, Lisa says today that if it wasn't for what had happened to her in her life, she wouldn't be where she is now. Positive things are happening for her that wouldn't be happening if she was still with her husband. She said these words with such a warm, sincere smile. Of course, she wishes that she and her children didn't have to go through this emotional trauma to get to the happy place they are now, but they've made it past the pain. She and her children are happier now than they've ever been. She's thankful that she found out when she did, rather than later. It just goes to show you, through the clouds, and through the darkness, the sun does shine again! At the same time, it shows that although Lisa and her children aren't a traditional family unit, they're doing just fine the way they are. They're better off without Lisa's husband, who was obviously dishonest and cold towards his family.

Even though Lisa felt that his revelation came without warning, it's clear that he must have had problems with his marriage for a long time, to prompt such a drastic move. While they weren't aware of it at the time, this unhappiness caused negative feelings throughout their family. Without him, they've learned to truly be themselves, and love each other completely. Lisa has been there for her children through all this hardship and they know they are completely loved.

***

My good friend Louise, who I've been close with since high school, has gone through a great deal of tragedy in her life. Unfortunately, Louise has lost many people in her life who were very important to her. When Louise was younger, her closest friend from high school died in a freak rock climbing accident. He was only twenty years old, and Louise was devastated. Shortly after that, she lost her father, who died due to a complication during surgery. Losing her father was incredibly difficult for Louise, but she managed to move past the pain and smile again.

Sadly, she faced even more misfortune. Louise had a very dear friend named Jeremy who was coming in to celebrate Louise's birthday up in Rockland County. Jeremy and Louise had been very close, and he had escorted Louise to my sister's wedding, even though he had never met my sister. Jeremy was a frequent flyer member and ALWAYS flew the same airline. However, shortly before his trip to Rockland County, another friend called Jeremy and asked if he would meet her in Pittsburgh before going on to Rockland County. Jeremy explained that he always flew with the same airline, and he already had his ticket. Well, Jeremy's friend finally convinced him to change his carrier and meet her in Pittsburgh. Jeremy never arrived . . . the plane tragically plunged from the sky, for no apparent reason, prior to landing in Pittsburgh. Jeremy had not originally planned to be on that plane but was destined to be there when he was. This was a horrible twist of fate for a person that was so full of life. I'll never forget the kind words he spoke on my sister's wedding video. He expressed such happiness for her and her new husband. He was a wonderful human being.

A few years later, Louise lost her sister-in-law Lisa during the attacks of September 11th. Lisa was just coming back from maternity leave that week, and had been arguing with her husband for weeks about going back to work. Lisa was determined to return to work, but her husband pleaded with her to stay home with their newborn baby boy and nearly two year old son. If only her husband won the argument, she would be here today. Louise's beautiful nephews were left without a mother, and Louise had lost yet another person that she loved. But Louise didn't lose her faith.

In the back of her mind, Louise always planned to adopt a baby from China. She told me, "I always planned on doing it and I always talked about it . . . ever since I can remember." Despite the tragedy she had faced in her life, she still had lots of love and compassion in her heart that she wanted to share with another person. She knew there were many little girls in China that needed loving families, and Louise had a strong desire to help one of these children. She didn't let the pain she had faced in her life stop her from helping others.

Louise has a close friend named Frank who was adopted when he was a baby, and discussing adoption with Frank helped to get the ball rolling. Right after her thirty-fifth birthday, she started the process. She kept it a secret from everyone for years until the time came for her to fly to China to finally meet her soon to be adopted daughter, Nora. It took her close to three years to adopt Nora, and Louise began the process about one year prior to her birth. It wasn't until Nora was fourteen months old that Louise was able to meet her and bring her home. It was a very long and arduous process, but Louise was willing to wait if it meant giving a loving family to an orphaned little girl.

Louise's Aunt Nadine accompanied Louise to China to meet her daughter for the first time. Louise boarded the plane from Chicago to Beijing with twelve other families who were going to adopt children at the same time. The families stayed in Beijing for two days before they flew to Munching where the orphanage was. The emotion on the ride to the orphanage was amazing; all thirteen families were speechless in anticipation. As soon as Louise got off the bus she saw Nora sitting on a bench . . . she just knew it was her. She felt an instant bond with her new daughter, but there was still business and paperwork to attend to before she could hold her new child.

All the families were taken into a big, cold room where they were given name tags that had their baby's American and Chinese names. Some of the couples were getting anxious and crying. Everyone had waited so long and traveled so far, the anticipation was almost too much. Louise told me she had been incredibly anxious through the entire trip. "The whole time there, I wasn't eating or sleeping . . . I think I lost twenty pounds in two weeks! On our last day in China, I thought I was going to faint." Now the time had finally come, Louise heard her agency's name called and she proceeded to the front. There, at the front of the room, was Nora. Louise's first thought was "Oh my God, I can't believe I have my baby!" After all her waiting, she finally got the chance to embrace her daughter.

All she could think was, "Let's get on with the paperwork and get back to the hotel so I can play with her!" Louise put her in a stroller and Nora started to play with her new toys. Louise immediately relaxed, and fell right into motherhood role. Everything felt completely natural, as if they had been together for years.

Louise couldn't believe what a wonderful match her and Nora are. All thirteen babies were matched up with their parents perfectly. Through a personal dossier which is a compilation of financial statements, letters of reference, an autobiography, a home study, letter of employment, medical background, and pictures, they come up with the perfect match. The agency took a lot of time matching the children with the right parents, to ensure the best situation for everyone.

The greatest part of the trip was when they actually landed on American soil. They had been told that as soon as the plane touched down in Chicago, the children would officially be American citizens. On the airplane, the pilot came across the loud speaker welcoming everyone to Chicago, and to the thirty babies on board, he said, "Congratulations! You're all American citizens." That was truly an emotional moment for Louise; she was finally home in her country with her new baby girl.

Louise told me, "I can't really explain the feeling when I first saw her. I fell in love. My first thought was 'I'm already in love with her, this is amazing.' When I saw her, it wasn't this uncomfortable or nervous feeling at all, it felt so natural. I couldn't be happier."

She told me she wishes that everyone could feel the joy that she's felt with Nora. She urges people to adopt if they have the opportunity. "To unite two people and give them both a better life is totally amazing!"

What's truly incredible is that Louise was able to love again despite all the tragedy in her life. She could have let life get her down, she could have become skeptical and introverted, but she didn't. She saw an opportunity to help someone, to share her love with someone, and she took it. She was determined to move forward with her life and be happy, and now she can't imagine being any happier. Nora has turned her world around and shown her that life does go on.

***

I've written a poem that encompasses my feelings on family and all that my family means to me.

Family Values

Through all our family lives, we endure so much

Whether it is joy, pain, or the thought of staying in touch

We often think of where we would be

If it wasn't for our family

Unfortunately some thoughts are more positive than others

For not all of us have loving fathers and mothers

And for those of us who've lost a family member

It is in our strongest prayers, the memories we wish to remember

It's so important to value your own family ways

With lots of hugs and kisses, and lots of praise

For it is within the home that we look for affection

From our spouses, our parents, our sibling connection

Families are what our world is made up of

The key to family happiness is unconditional love

So you must remain patient, understanding and kind

To have a family is treasure not everyone can find!

6

Friendship:
We're here for each other.

HAVING GOOD FRIENDS is an essential part of life. Having a good relationship with your family is wonderful, but having close friends, that's extra special. Friends are people who choose to love us and care about us, not because they're bound by blood and relations, but because they appreciate us for who we are. When I think about friendship, I like to think of it in these terms: A friend is someone who respects your opinion, enjoys your company, is happy for you when you feel good, and empathizes with you when you feel bad. A friend is someone you can have fun with, share your innermost thoughts with, and chat with for hours about everything and nothing. A friend accepts you for who you are, and allows you to completely be yourself, free of judgments.

Now think for a moment about hard it is to not only to find someone who fits all the above criteria but to actually be someone who fits those criteria, as well. To have good friends, you first have to be a good friend. Some people have no idea how important friendships are. Friendships are a fundamental part of life's happiness. Friends provide fun, companionship, support, and comfort. Life would be so lonely without the company of close friends.

People come in and out of our lives and some stay for a short period while others stay a lifetime. Sometimes what draws us to specific people doesn't make much sense. Did you ever have a friend that wasn't your type, and you find yourself saying, "Why are we even friends?" Well, it's a special connection that no one else could understand, but you and your friend might, and that's all that matters. It's just like with my sister and me. We have nothing in common, and yet she understands me better than anyone. Just because you and your friends are very different people with distinct personalities does not mean you can't respect those differences. A little controversy is sometimes the spice of life. How boring would life be if all your friends were just like you?

I don't believe in putting restrictions on the type of people I socialize with. It seems like many people only want to move within their own specific circles, and spend time with people just like themselves. Not me, I want to meet everyone! Friendship is such a beautiful thing, so the more, the merrier. Why limit yourself to people in the same walk of life? You already know people like that! I want new perspectives and points of view so I have friends of all types.

Friendship has no age limitations. I actually have friends that range from very young to over eighty years old. It's funny, when you're younger it is a rarity to have a friend so much older or younger than you. Now, as I see myself growing older, my friends' ages run the gamut. Not that someone's age really matters, age is just a number (and mine is unlisted!)

I have an eighty-two year old friend named Mary who happens to have the exact same eyes as my grandmother. In fact, when I asked my twin sister and my mother, "What do you see when you look into my friend Mary's eyes?" they both said "Grandma!" completely independent of each other. My grandmother and I were extremely close and I adored her. I believe I inherited my grandmother's faith and that she truly is my guardian angel who is guiding me through life. We connected in such a strong way. Some of my friends can't understand why I would be having coffee with an eighty-two year old woman, and they wonder what we could possibly have in common. Those kinds of thoughts seem shallow to me. Why concentrate on numbers? Look at the person, not their age. Spending time with Mary is just as valuable to me as spending time with any other friend that I adore.

All my friends hold a special place in my heart and they're all unique in their own way. They all have different levels of depth, some are more warm and fuzzy than others, some laugh more, and some cry more. One of my dreams is to have a room full of all my friends so that we all could intermingle, it would be such a great night out! We'd have a ball! I guess what I'm saying is, all my friends are special and unique in their very own way and I have such an appreciation for them. I cherish each and every friend I have.

Now, it may sound like I have so many friends, but compared to how many people I know, I really don't. It's not because I'm picky, because I have absolutely nothing to be picky about. I'm open to all people, and always willing to give anyone a chance. However, I choose my friends based on instinct. I listen to my inner voice, to that gut feeling inside of me, and I'm seldom wrong! Deep inside, I know if I will click with someone or not. Always trust your instincts. You know yourself better than anyone, and you know what kind of people you get along with.

My friend Melissa is someone who I knew I would get along with the moment I met her. We live in the same town, she's actually my neighbor, and we have children around the same age. However, fate has taken her life in a very different direction than mine. Melissa lost her husband in the 9/11 attacks. He didn't work in The World Trade Center, he normally worked out of offices in the midtown area. Unfortunately, he happened to have a meeting downtown that day. It is so overwhelming to try and comprehend the effect of that one day in history. So many lives were destroyed in mere moments, and our world was completely changed. It's surreal to imagine that each and every one of the people who died that day left behind a wife, a husband, sons, daughters, mothers, fathers, siblings, and so many more people in their circle of life. Now life continues on without them. It's a different world for each and every one of the families that have suffered the loss of a loved one. It's so painful to think about how, within minutes, their lives were changed forever. At the same time, it was quite comforting to hear about the magnanimity of all those who pulled together to help one another in their moment of need.

More than a year after 9/11, I asked my dear friend Melissa how many children in our kids' elementary school had lost parents in the terrorist attacks. I expected the answer to be at least twenty. She responded, "Just one . . . and it was my husband." There are 600 students in the school, and only my neighbor's children had lost a parent.

When I shared this with my husband and asked him what he thought he said without any hesitation, "You know Sue, you're here for a reason. You were meant to be her friend." As I always say, some things are meant to be, and I do feel that Melissa and I were meant to meet and become close, as a way to help her through her pain. Losing a spouse is so incredibly difficult, and without friends to support you and aid you through your grieving, it can seem like an impossible tragedy to move past. I think it's no coincidence that Melissa and I happened to meet, and I've been able to share my positive views with her.

You know, we just can't go it alone in this world. We need each other, and not only in dire cases, but always. We need love and companionship to feel complete as human beings. You cannot survive if you just rely upon yourself to get you through. There has to be either an outside source helping you through life, or at the very least, someone for whom you exist. We are on this earth to be cohabitants and to help one another. We do not truly exist for ourselves, but rather for everyone around us. That doesn't mean that we do not enjoy life if we are alone, but having others to care for gives us more reasons to enjoy our time here. Think about how often in life you do things not for yourself, but for those people that you love. The people around us motivate and encourage us, and give us a reason to keep going.

Where would we be without each other, without those who love and care for us? If only more people realized that it's O.K. to need other people, perhaps our world would be a happier place. It's a shame; it's viewed as a weakness in our society to need someone or to actually accept help from others. I guess most people's mentality is, "I don't need your help. I can do it myself." There's nothing wrong with being independent, but it's so important to still appreciate and accept support from others. If we refuse companionship, and think only about ourselves, the world becomes a very cold place.

I have a friend who recently went through some difficulties, and never would have made it through if she didn't accept the help and support of others. This friend of mine has gone through mental anguish that actually broke her to the point of needing professional medical help. I stood by her almost from afar because she would not let me into her world, out of fear that I would judge her and think less of her. She did not accept help easily; she wanted to go it alone because she was so skeptical about people and their reactions to her. Well, I stuck by her for over sixteen months until she came around and was well again. She was a friend of mine but I was not necessarily a friend of hers; she did not treat me as a friend, she held me at a distance. Yet I continued to treat her as a close friend because I understood that even though she did not want my help, she needed caring people around her. I stayed by her side as best I could without overstepping my bounds. I could see that things with her current doctor just weren't working, but she wasn't aware of it. Sometimes when you're so personally involved in a situation, you can't see things clearly, and you need a pair of outside eyes to give you an objective opinion.

Lo and behold, she finally listened to me after four months of severe suffering. As soon as she changed her doctor, it took three days for her to be well. Now why didn't she believe me sooner? Well, she took offense to me even recommending it. She wanted to do things her way, and didn't want anyone's advice or opinions. Her feeling was, "Who is she to tell me what doctor to go see, after all, I'm a nurse, I know much more about this stuff then she does." Well, logically, she was right. She did know quite a bit more than I about the medical field. But because she was looking at things from such a scientific point of view, she couldn't see them any other way. She couldn't see that her and this doctor just weren't meshing, and it wasn't going to work. She needed a friend who could look at the situation and give her an honest opinion.

I knew that until she got well, we would never culminate this friendship that I saw coming for over one and a half years. I could see that in her current state, she was too distrustful of people and couldn't become close with me, or anyone. I knew it would take a lot for her to be able to see me for who I really was.

Needless to say, my "new" friend changed her doctor and her situation improved. We now have a true friendship, and she's not afraid to let me be closer to her. The true glory was in seeing her well again, something she justly deserved after being through all that pain she suffered through for months. What's so interesting is that I never really got to meet the real her until now, because she was too wary of others to let me in. I knew the real person lay somewhere within all that pain and suffering, and I'm so glad I waited for her to emerge. There are reasons why life puts us in certain places at certain times, nothing is left to coincidence. We are meant to meet all these people in our lives for a reason.

***

"Live Like A Fried Egg . . . With Your Sunnyside Up!" That was my quote in my high school yearbook. On the day our yearbook information was due, I hadn't yet come up with a quote. I happened to be chewing a piece of Bazooka gum that morning, and the little fortune inside the wrapper had that incredible line. It was such a perfect way to describe my philosophy about life. There is no other way to live life; being positive makes life so much more enjoyable. Having the attitude that no matter what, everything is going to be ok, is one of the keys to happiness. I believed it then, and I believe it now. It's worked for me all these years.

I recently attended my twenty year high school reunion! It's amazing how time flies! It was such a blast from the past. I was overwhelmed with such emotion; I didn't know whether I should laugh or cry, I was just so happy! It's interesting how seeing everyone after so many years makes you realize that you don't think about how much people really mean to you until you've seen them again after so long. Absence really does make the heart grow fonder! I hadn't seen so many of these people for twenty years, and getting in touch with them again made me realize what an important part of my life they were.

Sometimes we don't make the effort to stay connected to those we love. Life seems to get in the way. We all have many responsibilities that we put at the top of our list, and old friends can fall to the bottom. You tell yourself, "I'll track them down soon and get in touch," and before you know it, you've been putting it off for twenty years!

Well, I took it upon myself to send out an email to every class member that had an email address listed in the directory, and boy, was I happy I did. The responses came in droves. We do need to stay connected to our past, for it is our yesterdays that have made us into who we are today. Each and every member of my high school class touched my life in some way during all those years of our childhood. There were a couple of our classmates who are now deceased, and I didn't find out about it until the reunion. I wish I had known. I definitely would have made the effort to either contact them prior to their passing or I would have paid my respects. It really made me realize how important it is to appreciate our friends while we have them. Cherish every moment you have with loved ones!

***

I truly believe that perception is reality. The way we view things effects how we react to our surroundings, and how we live our lives. If we have a positive outlook, our lives will be more positive. If you want to be happier, it's as simple as changing how you perceive things. Why not wake up every day thinking that your life is wonderful? Why not view your husband as the most amazing person in the world? Why not perceive your accomplishments in life to be monumental and fulfilling? Why not look at your life right now and say, "I am so blessed to be me!" Unfortunately, not everyone uses the power of perception in such a positive way. Many people perceive the world in very judgmental and skeptical ways, and it changes how they view those around them.

Sometimes in life, our perception of others gets in the way of actually getting to know who they really are. I attended a gathering with some friends of mine a while back and I can recall one of the ladies among us speaking badly about someone I actually admired. I saw my friend so differently than how the woman I was speaking to viewed her. Was there a rightful reason why she felt so negative toward my friend? Could my perception of my own friend be that skewed? Well, I used my logic. The woman she was speaking badly about volunteers a lot of her time helping children and attending school meetings. She is always looking to lend a helping hand and to make a difference. How could this person I just described be the same person that was being talked about in such a negative manner? If you see the good in people, you will perceive them for who they really are because everyone has goodness in them. Sadly, most people are guarded and have a hard time showing their true colors. These types of people, who feel uncomfortable being themselves and opening up to others, have trouble seeing the good in those around them. They just don't get close enough to people to get to know them. Their perception of the world is negative, and so it affects their lives in a negative way. They're too judgmental and skeptical to have close relationships.

Wouldn't it be great if we all just went about our lives not judging anyone, and got to know people before forming opinions? It's almost as if when people speak negatively about someone else, they think they're better than that person. They perceive themselves as being above everyone else. No one is better than anyone else on this earth. We are all created equal. However, no one is perfect and we should respect other people's point of views even though we may not share them.

Everyone is entitled to their own opinion, and we shouldn't infringe on their right to speak their minds, or judge them for what they believe. At the same time, we shouldn't let the opinions of others color how we behave. Some people are very sensitive to what other people think, and live their lives trying to impress the world around them. Too many times people forgo their own sense of being for the sake of someone else. The people in your life who really care about you, your family and your friends, don't care if your opinion is different than theirs, or if you look or act differently than they do. They love you for who you are, and for those things that make you unique. If you think about it, no true friend would want you to sacrifice yourself for them. They wouldn't want you to give up any piece of yourself or your individuality to try and make them happy or impress them.

I feel so blessed to be fulfilled in every aspect of my life including friends. I have such wonderful friends that I can be candid and honest with. They don't judge me or expect things from me, they're simply there to have fun and provide companionship. I am so fortunate to be able to have those special "girl talk" conversations with some of my dearest friends. Most women don't even know what they're missing when it comes to girlfriends. It seems that many women are very jealous and catty about other women, and have trouble maintaining sincere relationships with women. They view other women as a threat. I view my female friends as a blessing! I'm so glad to have wonderful women to talk to. Having girlfriends is a part of life that is so necessary. They let you talk about those things you can't talk about with anyone else; other people just wouldn't understand. Family members are sometimes too close to understand certain situations, and husbands don't want to discuss "girly" things.

Having girlfriends is like being a part of this circle of unconditional friends that you can be yourself with, chat with, and not have to explain yourself if you say something out of line or unintentional! It's so refreshing to be able to speak your mind and share your thoughts on a totally different level than you can with mere acquaintances. It's definitely not "Let's talk about the weather," conversations.

With my girlfriends I can express my most heartfelt concerns, or the mundane details of my day. It doesn't matter, they're there to listen and share. They're as close as family, yet it's completely different than being with family. There are no rules or concerns about being proper. We can just let loose and have fun! I went over to my friend's house one day and saw a plaque on her wall that read, "Friends Welcome, Relatives By Appointment Only." I thought it was hysterical, but she said, "Well my mother didn't see the humor in it!" That just made it funnier!

Humor is definitely one of those things that keep you going day after day. You can even find the humor in your own mistakes, in your own misunderstandings, in your own character flaws. That leads me to another one of my favorite expressions. "Excuses. Friends don't need them and enemies wouldn't believe them anyway!" I love this expression because it is so true. I don't really need to explain myself if I disappoint a friend or say the wrong thing. I would not do anything to harm them or say something hurtful to anyone, and my friends know that.

My point is, true friends can understand where you're coming from. You don't have to worry around them, or watch what you say. They know who you really are, and won't misconstrue your actions or words. It's so important to have people like that in your life. Imagine not ever being able to be candid, and having to keep your guard up all the time! What kind of life would that be?

It's all about caring and compassion. We need those things in our lives, and our friends open their hearts to us, not because they have to, but because they want to. I feel so blessed when someone opens up to me in that way, I do everything I can to reciprocate and be a good friend. It's not easy for people to let others into their lives, and we should truly appreciate it when someone trusts us enough to become a close friend. Some people have a very hard time doing that.

I remember a friend of mine who just had one disappointment after another with her friends. She would let people in to her life, and it wouldn't work out. It began to effect how she approached others. She said to me one day, "You know Susan, I only worry about what lies within my own four walls." It was almost as if she was really saying, "You know, I've had it with caring about others and concerning myself with outside things. I'm going to be more introverted and just worry about my own family. All I've gotten is complaints and grief for extending myself." That's what she truly feels, and I can understand why, but she shouldn't let a few bad situations change her outlook on life. Of course, it makes sense to be cautious when approaching new relationships, but you shouldn't close yourself off completely. We've all had rough situations in our lives, but if everyone retreated from society after a social disappointment, what kind of world would we have?

I view life so differently than she does. I feel like if someone needed my help I would lend a hand without a second thought, whether they were a friend or stranger. I don't worry about whether or not that person would do the same for me. I won't let someone else's negative outlook stop me from being compassionate. As a society, if we just look outside our own four walls more often and reach out more to those in need, what a better world it would be!

***

The wonderful thing about friends is that they provide you with other points of view that you wouldn't normally get to experience. They help you see things from new perspectives, and often you find yourself experiencing things you never would have tried if you didn't have your friends urging you toward new ideas.

During my freshman year of college, when I was nineteen years old, I was preparing to go on spring break with some of my friends. I had planned to travel with my friend Louise, the woman I spoke about earlier in the book who adopted a daughter from China. We were close friends even back in college. Louise's sister was going to spend the break in Fort Lauderdale, but we had very different plans. Louise and I were going skiing in Vermont with the Ski Club, and our friend Carly was going to spend spring break at home. The day our break started, we were driving away from school and I JOKINGLY said, "Florida, here we come!" Carly was in the back seat and she was just planning to go home to a suburb outside of Syracuse, and Louise and I had already put our deposit down on our Vermont trip.

Well, Carly turned to Louise and said, "Wouldn't it be great if we just picked up and drove down to Florida?!" Louise looked at her like she was nuts. Louise was much more conservative than we were. I, however, believe in living for the moment! Without a second's hesitation, I said to Carly, "Let's go!" Well, long story short, within an hour, we were packed and driving down to Florida!

Obviously we didn't have a lot of time to plan, and as we were on our way we realized that Carly didn't know how to drive my stick shift car. So, when it was Carly's turn to drive, I got between the two front seats and maneuvered her to fourth gear. Carly was then able to drive for hours on a straightaway, while I catnapped in the back seat! I wasn't going to let any little obstacles stand in the way of our vacation! Then, somewhere in Georgia, we hit another bump in the road. One of our tires went flat, and we couldn't afford a new one. It seemed like it could be the end of our journey. We pulled into a gas station and asked the guy to put the donut on. We drove thousands of miles on this donut that was supposed to be temporary! It all worked out fine.

Being on the road with my two close friends was such a wonderful experience. It was literally a laugh a minute. I don't know what was better, the ride down or the vacation itself. When we finally ended up at the strip in Fort Lauderdale, we all looked at each other in total amazement. The place was one big college party; it was a far cry from what we had originally planned in Vermont! Now, at this point, Louise's sister was already in Fort Lauderdale but we had no idea where she was staying. We hoped we would be able to find accommodations somewhere and call her mom to find out where Louise's sister was staying, so we could hook up with her.

As we neared the end of the strip, we pulled into this very nice hotel, hoping they'd have a room for the night, and just so happened to get a spot right by the pool deck. The next thing we knew, there were some guys hanging off the pool deck making fun of my ski rack. "Oh girls, don't you think you're in the wrong state to be driving around with a ski rack?!" If they only knew the story!

We got out of the car and started to walk across the parking lot to see if there were any vacancies in the hotel, when suddenly Louise's sister walks right up to us. "Hey guys, what are you doing here?! Aren't you supposed to be skiing?"

It was a scene right out of a movie! Not only did we find Louise's sister, Amy, we couldn't believe she was staying at the very hotel we pulled into! Now, what are the chances of that?? We ended up staying with Amy because all the rooms were sold out. If we hadn't found her, we wouldn't have had any place to stay! Needless to say, this was the beginning of one very memorable vacation that none of us will ever forget.

At the end of our Ft. Lauderdale excursion, we made it back to college in about twenty-six hours, just in time for school the next day. Everyone was wondering how we got such incredible tans from a ski vacation! We had the best spring break vacation ever, and I never would have gone if it weren't for my friends.

Life is all about timing. The timing of this trip was impeccable. What were the chances of us running into Amy at the very same hotel she was staying in, as soon as we arrive in Fort Lauderdale, more than twenty hours after leaving our college campus in upstate New York? All these coincidences are really signs that everything is just meant to be, that everything will work out as long as you believe it will. When we first started talking about the trip, Louise thought we were crazy! But as we made our way there, and everything began to work itself out, we all realized that it wasn't so crazy after all! Louise never would have done something so impulsive, but with a little nudge from some friends she trusted, she had an amazing vacation that we'll all be telling our grandchildren about one day.

***

I have this friend whose name just so happens to be the same as mine, Sue. Sue and I live what we both call "parallel lives." We met on the ball field one day because our sons happen to be on the same baseball team. She heard someone mention Fred and Sue. Well, this made her ears perk up because her brother's name is Fred and her name is Sue, and seeing that she only had one sibling, she very rarely heard the two names in combination except from within her own family. Her father's name is Fred and my husband's father's name is Fred. Her son is named Nicholas Frederick. My son's name is Frederick Nicholas. We both have the same OB/GYN. We both had our children at North Shore University Hospital in Manhasset. Our sons are one week apart, Frederick Nicholas was born on March 17th and Nicholas Frederick was born on March 10th, both Pisces. My friend Sue is a Gemini and married a Capricorn. I am a Capricorn and married a Gemini. My wedding anniversary is June 5th. Sue's wedding anniversary is June 4th. It's uncanny.

One day, Sue and I attended Field Day at the elementary school and both our sons, within minutes of each other, lost the very same tooth on the playground during Field Day festivities! It's incredible how many of these "coincidences" occur in our lives. Of course, I don't view them as coincidences; I believe they're things that happen for a reason. It just doesn't make sense that there could be so many coincidences; it has to be part of a bigger plan. All of us have a function in life, we have a place. When we recognize that these "coincidences" are really signs of where we're meant to be and what we're meant to do, everything falls into place. What are the chances that I meet this woman with the same name, who has so much in common with me, and lives so close to me, and has a child who gets along wonderfully with my children? We were meant to meet each other, to provide support and companionship for each other to help us get through this adventure called life.

I'm so blessed to have a friend like Sue. Our bond goes far beyond simply having things in common. We get along so amazingly well, we've never even had an argument or disagreement of any kind. Sue swears that she must really be my sister, and we were just separated at birth. She truly feels like a sister to me, that's how strong our friendship is. Friends can be a second family to you, and they're a family you get to choose!

What's amazing about life is we cannot exist without each other. We need to need, we need to want, and we need to desire the company of those we love. That is living. To exist alone without anyone we love in our lives is a sad existence, but to live with those we love is what life is all about. Too many people are held back because of pride, the fear of making a mistake, or concern about how people will judge you. All these things can get in the way of having close relationships. As the saying goes, life often gets in the way of life. It's up to each and every one of us to make sure we make a conscious effort to minimize this interference and appreciate life without all those concerns holding us down. We need to bond with people, and develop relationships without fear. Yet, at the same time, you and only you can make your existence as fun and as exciting as you want it to be.

The people around us enhance our experiences, but they are not responsible for our lives. We must still make the effort to live a healthy, positive life; we can't expect our friends and families to do everything for us. It is up to us to face the world with a positive outlook every day, only then can we truly be happy. Having good friends makes it easier to keep that optimistic attitude. It's all in how you view the world around you. Only you can have the vision to see the light behind the darkest clouds. Only you can make a difference in your day. Only you can share your love, free of the fear of not being loved back. It's worth the risk! Open your heart to those around you.

7

Career:
Why not enjoy what you do for a living?

IT'S SO IMPORTANT to have a purpose in life. Of course, our main purpose is to better our world and help those around us, but it's nice to have something more concrete, that we experience every day. It's good to have something that drives you to keep going, something that gives you a reason to wake up in the morning. Many of us have families and children which motivate us on a daily basis. We go to work each day to support our families and ourselves, and we work hard to do it.

Most people see work as a chore, a necessity that they don't enjoy. I think that's so sad. Going to work is something that almost every adult has to do, so why should it be so miserable? Think about how much of your life you spend at work. Do you really want to waste that much of your time being unhappy? I know what you're thinking. You don't have a choice. But you do!

I love what I do for a living, and I'm driven to keep doing better work. As I was growing up, I acknowledged my gifts. I paid attention to what I was good at and what I enjoyed. I realized that the path to happiness was finding a career in which I could use my gifts. By following my dreams and staying true to myself, I was able to follow the career path I desired.

I enjoy problem solving. That's what I do best, and I love it. I also like working with numbers; so put these two areas of interest together and you have one happy market researcher! I specialize in the area of market research survey design and methodology design. I have an innate understanding of how to approach any market research proposal from an optimal standpoint. For me, it's like doing a puzzle; it's challenging, but fun. The purpose of my job is to solve marketing informational needs for major companies to help them save money and satisfy customers. Basically, I design and conduct surveys to tell companies what their customers want.

I was doing this type of work for publishing companies, working in-house. After I had my first son, I attempted to use the childcare program supplied by my company, so I could continue working. Unfortunately, it just didn't work out. I decided to try working from home, and so I started freelancing my services as a market researcher in the publishing industry. Before I knew it, I had several reputable magazine publishers calling me, asking me to conduct a variety of different primary research studies. When I began my freelance business, I was outsourcing most of my services, hiring other companies to do some of the research work. However, I experienced a lack of quality control that I felt was integral to me and my clients. I felt my clients were spending good money on my services, and I was responsible for delivering accurate information. I believe that if I'm going to do work for someone, I might as well make it worth THEIR while. In other words, do what you know is going to wow your employer or your clients. This is no dress rehearsal, so go after that job and make it purposeful. So, I thought it would be best if I was directly involved in all facets of my business. As they say, if you want something done right, you have to do it yourself.

I eventually took all aspects of marketing research in-house and my company grew to about a forty person call center/market research firm. My success came from doing the right thing and charging the right price. Every penny I made my first year I put back into the business. I purchased forty cubicle stations, one for each of my phone interviewers. When I purchased the cubicles, I made sure the desk space was sufficient enough for a cup of coffee and perhaps a snack, as well as the employees' paperwork. I made sure I bought the most comfortable chairs with arms because I knew that my employees were going to be sitting for hours at a time. I purchased the chair with the widest seat to make sure those employees who might be on the heavier side were as comfortable as possible. When I purchased the head sets, I didn't buy the cheap $30 ones, I spent $150 on the phone system for each interviewer, to ensure they had the best quality equipment. There was something called noise cancellation headsets which allowed the interviewer to not be distracted by any background noise, and they kept the person being interviewed from hearing the noise of the other interviewers in the background. I spent the extra money on these to make the work experience more pleasant for my employees.

I follow the philosophy of "Do unto others as you would like others to do unto you." I wanted to make sure that my employees had the best working environment that I could provide. How could I expect them to do good work for our company if I didn't make the effort to treat them well? My husband was baffled by how much money I spent on the little things. I let him know that I wanted to treat my employees as well as I could. I also paid my employees 20% more than my competitors because I truly believe your employees are the backbone of your company. There was no shaving or cutting corners anywhere.

Well, we were off and running. I sold our services to some of the biggest magazine publishers in the world. Why were we so successful? Because we delivered on our promise, at a reasonable price, without sacrificing quality. We became successful overnight. My company was not only about satisfying my customers; it was about satisfying my employees. It had to start with the employees, because without them, the company would be nothing. Due to the dedication of every employee in my market research firm, we were involved in some of the most important market research projects in the industry.

My career has been very rewarding, and I'm so thankful for that. I was involved in some of the earliest customer satisfaction studies for the Sony Corporation when they first entered the PC market. I worked closely with the Director of Marketing to find out what their customers thought about their newly purchased PCs. This research helped to shape future PC products designed by Sony, including both their laptop as well as their desktop division. What a thrill to be able to tell Sony, before they themselves knew, how their users felt about their product, and how to improve upon their product and services. It's just an amazing field. My slogan is "The Wonderful World of Research." I guess that pretty much tells you how I feel about my career!

I was very fortunate to break into this field straight out of college. I had friend whose sister worked for PC Magazine, and she helped me find a job doing market research for developing technologies, at a time when new technology was being developed at a breakneck pace. I've had so many wonderful and exciting experiences. I've met incredible people who have gone on to impact the way all of us live our daily lives. I met Philippe Kahn of Borland, and Peter Norton of Norton Utilities was in our professional social circles. My boss introduced me to Eckert Pfeiffer, the CEO of Compaq Computers, at a time when people didn't even know what Compaq was, let alone how to spell it! I even met Bill Gates at COMDEX in Las Vegas in 1989. I met Michael Dell, the founder of Dell Computers, and I was present for the unveiling of his advertising campaign to launch his product line for the very first time! I met with the Gateway executives as we laughed over the reason behind the cow print boxes. I met with IBM executives to discuss whether the 386 chip should be installed in their laptops. I analyzed primary research for the very first black computers, intended to replace the industrial putty colored ones. I worked with 3Com, IBM, Microsoft, Intel, Gateway, Compaq, Novell, and many more.

All this happened within the first year of my career; it was like an incredible roller coaster ride, one thrill after another! It was a great time in history that changed the way we do business today. Networks, LANs, Databases, customer-relationship management software, ATM, E-commerce, you name it, I lived it!

Having a career that I love has helped make my life so much more fulfilling. It makes me feel useful, accomplished and worthwhile. I attribute my success to acknowledging my God given gifts, and following my heart. We've all been given our own unique gifts, and we must nurture them. If you look inside yourself and accept your own natural gifts, you, too, can be an amazing success. Don't ignore your gifts, cherish and cultivate them.

What if F. Scott Fitzgerald didn't realize he was gifted as an author? What if Frank Sinatra didn't realize he was gifted as an entertainer? What if surgeons who perform miraculous surgeries and save lives every day never realized they were gifted in the art of healing? We were given these gifts for a reason, for a higher purpose. Think about it. Where did these talents come from? It's not always genetics! Look at Michael Jordan's father, he was no Michael Jordan. Look at Barbara Streisand's mother, she was no Barbara Streisand. They were given incredible abilities that their parents didn't have. You have to believe the gifts we have are given to us for a reason, and the reason each of us are given these gifts is to better mankind.

When we nurture and use our talents, not only will we be happier, but we will spread that positive energy. All of our gifts are meant to help the world in some way, even if you can't see the effect right away. It's like a domino effect. Look at Oprah Winfrey, her inspiration alone has helped millions of people. She had a talent, and she followed her dreams. At first, it may not have seemed that she could help others with her gift, but eventually it became clear to everyone what her purpose was. She touches so many people in such a positive way. This is what happens when you acknowledge your unique abilities. It leads you toward your calling.

***

Usually, the feeling of success comes with doing something you love, something you are passionate about, something you believe in. It's so important to have direction in your life, and to only move forward instead of staying stagnant. Sure, the idea of not working sounds nice at first, but what would you do all day if you didn't have something to work for? How would you feel if you didn't go into the office, or you didn't take care of your children? You'd start to get bored, and depressed. With nothing to do, you'd begin to feel useless and lazy. Having some type of career or daily purpose makes us feel accomplished, and that is such a vital aspect of life. It is one of the best feelings one can ask for!

We must set our individual goals and try to achieve them day in and day out. It gives us something to keep reaching for, a reason to keep going. Along the way, we must work for the greater good. Never take a job that you feel violates your moral principles. You will never be happy if you feel you're contributing to an unworthy cause. Try to find time in your busy schedule to help with charitable organizations, or community activities, because that is just as valuable a purpose as any career. I often find myself involved in a variety of causes that range from being on community committees, sitting on the board of my Women's Club or just helping with fundraising for charity events that regularly take place in my community.

For those of us who work to make ends meet, we must approach our jobs with pride and with purpose. Most of us go through life looking at our jobs as a means of putting food on the table or paying our bills and that's really not such a positive approach to working. Since we spend the majority of our time working, we must find those positions that fulfill us.

We must not come home at night dreading going to work the next day. It is up to each and every one of us to make a difference in our own lives. I often think about how so many people are unhappy with their jobs when they are pretty much solely responsible for choosing what path they take.

A friend of mine named Sally is a single parent who has been working for many years to support her family. She was a very successful producer but dreaded going to work each and every day because her boss was far from pleasant to work with. I had seen Sally a while ago and she explained to me how unbearable work was becoming. I could see the pain in her face. The same person who, when I first met her, had pep in her step, was now looking more like a person with her chin on the ground. I told Sally, "You must get out of your situation, what an awful way to live." She replied that she had to keep this job because it was financially secure for her. She was a single mom, and therefore the only breadwinner for the family.

Well, lo and behold, shortly after I ran into Sally and we spoke about her possibly getting another job, her boss let her go because business was just too slow. Fortunately, he offered her a little severance package to help her along until she got on her feet freelancing for another company. As the saying goes, when one door closes, another opens. For Sally, this was a scary time, but she has faith that things will work themselves out. As fate would have it, she lost her job and was literally forced to look elsewhere. While it was difficult at first,

Sally is relieved that she no longer has to work in such a miserable environment. She realizes that she is definitely better off and that through her perseverance she will find a better job. She knows not to view it as a negative situation, but rather, as an opportunity to find a new, better position.

Sally held on to a miserable job to maintain her lifestyle and pay her monthly bills. It's easy to get comfortable in situations where the money is secure, but many times we risk our happiness for such security. In situations where you choose a position or a career, you must never sacrifice your well-being for any amount of money. Those who make good money but are not satisfied with their jobs are only fooling themselves into believing that they are living fulfilled lives. In most cases, job satisfaction correlates with life happiness. Though it's important to try and leave work problems at work, they eventually do seep into your everyday home life. Work is such a huge part of our lives that if you're unhappy with work, the rest of your life will suffer. So don't tell yourself you're going to stay in a horrible job because you need the job security. The reality is, in this day and age, most jobs really aren't secure, anyway. It is really a false sense of security, because most companies don't think twice about letting someone go to cut costs or trim the fat. Why not go after a position you know you can succeed at and you know you will enjoy? Why sacrifice your happiness?

***

When my husband Fred began his career in advertising at the early age of twenty-two years old, he thought it was a good career choice. He soon found out that it wasn't the right place for him. He was unhappy, and he knew he was destined for other things, but he had to take the necessary steps and follow his dreams if he wanted to be happy.

Fred came from a family of successful, independent businessmen, and wanted to try to work in "the real world" for a while before attempting to strike out on his own. Fred came from a long line of entrepreneurs; it was really in his blood. Back in the early 70s, Fred's dad met a chemist in California who was making products for the first manufacturer of toilet bowl cleaners. Poppy saw a potential career; he realized that they could make other household cleaning chemicals, as well. He started private labels that were equivalent to national brands, basically store brand versions of other products. He provided private label products for some of the biggest retail chains in history, such as Woolworth's and McCrory's, and eventually he broke into drug store chains, wholesalers, and distributors. They were pioneers in the area of private label household cleaning chemical manufacturers. This was an extremely successful company. In fact, the Woolworth Window Clear was outselling the national brand window cleaner. Fred's father made a great success out of a company he had started from scratch.

Fred's mom was a Reingold model and was actually the famous Norman Rockwell Fountain Girl for Coca Cola. She was in ads that ran nation-wide, and made the cover of many of the top selling magazines. The entrepreneurial spirit in Fred's family doesn't stop there. His Uncle Nino, along with his father, manufactured the first frozen pizza. Pop would sell the product to the owners of the biggest grocery chains in the North East. They became so successful that General Foods bought out Nino's Pizza for a pretty penny. Fred's Uncle Dick continued his career in frozen foods and represented one of the first frozen food producers in the grocery trade. Uncle Dick eventually started his own brokerage firm, specializing in frozen foods, under the company name Ferrari Marketing. Fred's Uncle John, an electrical engineer who graduated from Colombia University, began his career working with Lionel Trains. He was one of the top employees, and was influential in designing Lionel Trains. Uncle John now owns his own manufacturing company in New Jersey, specializing in power supplies and transformers.

Fred decided to give advertising a try, considering his mother's former career. He thought it would be a challenging and creative career choice. It made sense. When Fred started his career as an assistant buyer in an advertising agency, he would go to work appearing as though he should be running the agency. He was polished and very business savvy. That's all he knew. He came from a family of entrepreneurs, people who had created their businesses from the ground up through hard work and professionalism. That's just the way his mind worked. He had a natural way of directing others and delegating responsibilities. Well, that did not fly very well at the ad agency! As an assistant buyer, Fred was supposed to take orders, not give them!

He was basically a fish out of water. He was a natural leader and businessman, it was in his blood to run things and have control over all aspects of the business. He would watch the ad sales staff come in to pitch spots to the major networks and he would grow frustrated that he couldn't be more hands-on with the sales. What Fred didn't realize is that his business sense was part of his makeup; it was something he couldn't ignore. He just wasn't happy. It was not the money, because even though he started off making basically nothing, he knew he would be able to climb the ranks pretty quickly. It was a matter of overall satisfaction. He didn't feel challenged; he didn't feel that this was his place. He knew he had other skills that weren't being utilized. He wanted to make use of his abilities, he wanted to grow as a professional, and he knew this wasn't the place where that would happen.

Shortly after leaving the ad agency, Fred began working with his father. He had been around his father's business all of his life, and had actually attended a number of trade shows with his dad as a child, so he was very familiar with the inner workings of the business. Fred eventually started his own company, under the same name his dad had first used many years ago, Horizon Brands International, Inc. Fred is responsible for all U.S. sales for a Canadian manufacturer of health and beauty aids. He happened to meet the owners at one of his Dad's trade shows and decided to convince this manufacturer to rely on him to bring their products to the United States, and the rest is history.

Fred has been with this Canadian manufacturer now for about ten years. Fred began doing at an early age what most men don't accomplish until their fifties. His clients are often amazed at how he got where he is through the help of his father's teachings and motivation, as well as his drive to succeed. Fred is still one of the youngest in his industry, selling to some of the biggest retail chains in the country. The point of the story is, you have to find your own comfort level. Find a job that you're happy at, and don't settle for less. Know what you're good at and don't sell yourself short. If you go after what you know you can accomplish, then you will succeed.

It was never about the money for Fred, it was the thrill of the hunt. Getting into accounts he never was able to penetrate before, satisfying all his clients, that's what Fred's mission was. In fact, most of the time, Fred has no idea what kind of money he makes because he doesn't ever stop to ask, he just keeps going. Fred is a perfect example of working for the good of working and being successful. He does something he enjoys, and it keeps him going, day after day.

***

I recently stepped into a very popular salon in my hometown and I asked to speak to the owner. I had witnessed something that was so disturbing that I thought as a responsible citizen, I should make the owner aware of what was happening. It turned out there was this one employee who is undergoing serious psychological problems and her illness is effecting employee satisfaction all around her. It is so apparent that this employee has no qualms about speaking in a derogatory manner to her fellow employees in front of customers.

When I spoke to the owner, he was very apologetic towards me but didn't seem too concerned with the effect this troubled employee had on his other employees. His philosophy was "the customer comes first."

I said to him, "No, the employee comes first, the customer comes second." If you don't create a comfortable, trusting, secure environment for your employees, then the atmosphere for your customers is not going to be pleasant. I, myself, felt very uneasy around this troubled employee but the owner didn't seem to do anything about how this woman treated her fellow workers. I explained to him that employee satisfaction usually means customer satisfaction; it's like a trickle down effect.

It is not only for our own fulfillment that we work. It is for the good of the organization, our co-workers, the clients, and so on. When you are part of an organization, you must consider all those people that you affect through your work. Be considerate of those around you, both the customers and your co-workers. If you're in a position of power, consider the feelings of your employees and make their work environment as pleasant as possible. If people are not happy with their jobs, they will not produce good work. Make your employees enjoy their time at work, and they'll be happy to do their best for the company. It's just like any other aspect of our lives. Treat people well, and they'll return the favor.

I had a far more pleasant experience at a different salon not to long ago. I had been shopping for groceries, and I noticed that a few doors down from the bagel place was a nail salon that I used to visit. I think the last time I was there was on my wedding day. When I walked in, among all the women working there, I recognized the woman who used to do my nails, Lilly. I hadn't seen her in about ten years! I asked how she was, and she told me that she now owned the nail salon! It's funny, I wasn't a bit surprised. She is a lovely woman who truly deserves good fortune and there's been such a difference in the salon since she's become the owner. A woman I was sitting next to happened to be coming in for more than ten years and she said the salon is a much more peaceful place since Lilly took over. I can see why. She's just such a pleasant person, and the whole salon reflects her temperament, quiet and peaceful. I guess it's strange to say now, knowing that she's the owner, but I somehow knew that was going to be the case. She always seemed so kind and dedicated to her work. She was so good with the customers, it was clear she would make a good owner. It's amazing, Lilly started out in that salon doing nails, and through hard work and persistence, she now owns it!

***

The other day I took my sons to get their hair cut at the same place they've been going since the very first time they had their hair cut. I've known the hairdresser, Louis, for about eleven years now. He takes such pride in his work. I call him the Picasso of hair design. He is definitely gifted in this area. He does hair for many celebrities, yet he's always so humble, never stuck up. He still makes time for me and my boys. My niece, Alyssa, says she won't go anywhere else to have her hair cut, and my two boys agree. They love this place; children really do have good instincts! We travel three towns over just to see Louis, and my niece travels about thirty minutes from where she lives to have him cut her hair.

Louis is extremely dedicated to his career. His purpose in life goes beyond just cutting people's hair. Some people would see it as a superficial career, but what they don't realize is, it's about making people feel good. Louis really is fulfilled all day long when he watches his clients leave his chair and they are so happy with their hairstyles. He knows he's done more then just make them look nice, he's made them feel better about themselves.

The amazing thing about Louis is he sincerely knows that money is not the answer to happiness. All day long, he listens to his clientele talk about all their material possessions. They talk about what trips they're going on, what new gadgets they've bought, what designer clothing they love, things like that. Louis time and time again replies, "That's nice." He thinks it's wonderful that his clients find joy in going on vacations and obtaining beautiful things; however, he knows that this isn't the real key to happiness. He realizes that most of those people who talk this way probably aren't very happy; they're trying to create joy in their lives by buying expensive things. He knows that doesn't work, that eventually the novelty wears off.

Louis realizes that no worldly possession can replace the love he receives from his family and close friends. He talks to so many people each day, and he learns a lot from listening. He sees that money isn't making people happy. He hears the difference between someone who is truly satisfied with their life, and someone who is searching for more by buying expensive things. He knows that he doesn't have the kind of money that most of his clients have, but that doesn't matter to him. He takes pride in his work and just appreciates every day.

Of course, Louis appreciates nice things, just like everyone else. But the difference between Louis and most of his clients is that he does not rely on those material possessions to find happiness. He receives fulfillment every day by watching another happy customer leave his chair. Louis takes pride in his work and enjoys it day in and day out. He gets so much pleasure from making people happy. Louis doesn't need those fancy cars or high lifestyles to enjoy his every day life. He's more fulfilled doing what he does and having the family he has to support him. He's better off than most of those people who have enough money to buy the salon he works in!

Louis is happy with his life because he has a career that satisfies him. He feels he is doing something to help others, and at the same time, he's being true to himself. He is very gifted at what he does, and it's something he's always enjoyed doing. He followed his dream, rather than giving into the pressures of others. He doesn't care that he could be making more money doing something else; it's not about money for him. This is what he loves to do, and when you do what you love, you will be fulfilled. It's so nice to see Louis. I am so fond of him that I go to visit on a monthly basis. He really has a way of giving you a reality check!

We often drift in the direction that our natural talents lead us. We find jobs that utilize the skills that we're good at. Our abilities are a large factor in our success at the jobs that we choose. That's one side of it. Being good at what you do is essential. The other side is that you have to enjoy what you're good at. You have to embrace your talents and use them towards a career that you can be happy with. When you put both of these scenarios together you end up having a job where you feel good about yourself.

8

<u>Kindness:</u>
Following your heart makes all the difference in the world!

WHEN I WAS pregnant with my second son, my first born Freddy was only a toddler. He came over to me, looked at my big, pregnant belly, and asked, "Mommy, how will your heart be big enough to love me and the new baby?" I smiled and told him that mommies have hearts that are big enough for all their children. He seemed to be quite content with that answer. He knew that I would always love him, no matter how many children I had.

We don't usually think about it, but it is amazing how our hearts are big enough to encompass all the love we come across in our lives. There is no maximum capacity. You can never have too much love in your life, or too much empathy or compassion. Our hearts just grow bigger and bigger as we need them to. So why not love as much as you can? Why not be kind to everyone you meet? It certainly won't hurt you . . . I guarantee your heart can handle it!

A friend of mine asked me recently, "Why are we here? For what, all this pain and suffering?"

My response to her was, "We're here to make the world a better place." For me, it's a no brainer. We've been given this capacity to care and to love for a reason. We, as humans, have been given gifts that no other creature on this planet has. We have these gifts for a purpose, to care for the world around us. We've been entrusted with this earth, and given free will and the power to change our surroundings. We are the caregivers of God's creations. Think about it, if everyone approached life with this one goal in mind, how much more wonderful would this world be?

Now, how often do you hear people complaining about their own woes and they can't look beyond their own nose? It's ok to be concerned about the troubles in your life, but at the same time you need to look around and see that there are many people who have it much worse. We should appreciate what we have, and help those who are not so fortunate. The beautiful thing is that when we help others, we help ourselves. It's a wonderful cycle. If you help other people to be happier and healthier, then you'll live in a more positive and optimistic world. Your surroundings affect your lifestyle, so why not help improve the world around you?

I would help a stranger like I would help a friend. I walk this earth as if we are all God's children and we are here to help each other and to coexist in harmony. I think all neighbors have the inkling that they would like to reach out and help each other but no one ever does. Most neighbors don't even converse. A nod, or a quick "Hi, how are you?" is mostly what you get. However, if there is someone in need, neighbors are usually the first ones to offer a hand. So why don't we offer that helping hand or extra hello when people don't need it? Why only be kind in dire circumstances? That's a good question. It's very rare that people go out of their way to help unless they think it's a grim situation. But the effort behind being neighborly is so much easier than the effort it takes to be enemies. Time and time again you hear people complain about their neighbors. What a sin! You are put here to coexist in the same neighborhood and your first feelings should be welcoming, not skeptical.

One of my friends used to tell me she loved to introduce me as "her neighbor who was her friend", not "her friend who was her neighbor." Now, don't lose me here! She explained that she loved the fact that we were neighbors who were also good friends because she felt that it was so special that she had a close friend in me. She knew how rare it was for neighbors to actually become genuine friends, and we both cherish each other's friendship.

***

Sometimes people are too hard on themselves. It seems like when you have high expectations for yourself, you often impose those expectations on the people around you. Life would be so much more enjoyable if people were just more accepting of themselves and of others. It's O.K. to make mistakes. It's O.K. not to do the "right thing" every time. It's O.K. to lose your patience. It's O.K. to admit you're wrong. It's O.K. to say you're sorry. It's O.K. to show your true feelings. It's O.K. to help someone in need when you feel the world around you doesn't care. It's O.K. to call a friend you've neglected to call for an exorbitant amount of time. It's O.K. to rekindle frayed relationships. It's O.K. to be understanding even though you may not necessarily agree. It's O.K. to be you! If you just follow your heart and do what you feel is right, then it all is going to be O.K. It's all about listening to your heart and being true to yourself.

When you are true to yourself, and live life the way you enjoy it, you're automatically living in a more positive zone. You're happier and more confident when you follow your instincts and listen to your heart. Your optimism and joy will have a ripple effect among your friends. Don't you always feel better when you're around someone who is happy? Think about the saying "misery loves company." Pessimism breeds more pessimism. If you walk around being negative, you're going to find yourself surrounded by negative people and negative events. So be optimistic, and see how quickly things start to get better.

People are naturally attracted to positive energy. My friends tell me that when I walk into a room, the whole place lights up. I often feel that I have an inner glow that everyone can see. It seems like people just get cheerier when they're around me. I'm contagious!

***

Even though I've had rough patches in my life, I feel blessed every day. Every life has its ups and downs, but I find that as long as I stay upbeat, things work themselves out.

A few Christmases ago, I received a gorgeous diamond cross pendant from Santa. As I went to the bank to put it in my safety deposit box for safekeeping, I realized I didn't have it with me. When I first got to the bank, I ran into Connie, one of my good friends from my old neighborhood, and we began chatting. After a few minutes, I just couldn't help myself; I had to show Connie the necklace. "Look what Santa brought me!" I said, as I reached into my bag. Well, the necklace wasn't there!

I looked through my handbag and my pockets and it was nowhere to be found. I recalled that the day before I had brought my son Freddy to the Tennis Academy for his lessons. While I was there, I took some time to admire my beautiful necklace, which was still in the box at the time. Well, during Freddy's tennis lesson, my son TJ and I sat in the bleachers overlooking the court. We were chatting, and by mistake, TJ had knocked over my bag, and all its contents fell underneath the small metal bleachers. Everything in my bag spilled out and things were scattered all over the ground. I picked up what I thought was everything, forgetting I had the box with the diamond cross in my bag.

As I stood there in the bank with Connie, I thought to myself, when my bag spilled under the bleachers, the necklace must have been on the floor and I didn't see it! In fact, I didn't even think to look for it. Of course, Connie was concerned that I had lost the necklace, but I knew things would be fine and it would show up. The teller overheard our conversation and said, "Wow, that's great that you have such a positive attitude, I hope you find it!" What she didn't understand was that I was positive because I knew I would find the necklace.

I went straight to my office, which was located down the road from the bank. I called over to the Tennis Academy and explained to the receptionist what had happened. Half way through my story she said, "Don't worry, I have it here, safe at the reception area." I asked her the name of the person who turned it in. It turned out to be another parent who just happened to notice it under the bleachers.

So how did I know I would find it? Think about it . . . if you found the necklace, wouldn't you turn it in? I know I would. I have faith in the good will of others. I believe that given the chance, people will do the right thing. So when I lost the necklace, my gut instinct told me to trust in others to do the honest thing and turn the necklace in. What's even more amazing is that the person who turned it in didn't do it for a reward or anything in return. She did it because it was the right thing to do.

There are a few things I instilled in my children since birth and one of the most important is to be kind and loving to all around you. Though the world is filled with hatred, there are many beautiful people in it. You should give everyone a chance, instead of walking into a situation assuming the worst. We're on this earth together, to help each other, understand each other, and give of ourselves. It is in the giving that we receive. Being good to others is its own reward; we receive the peace of mind that comes from knowing we helped make the world a little bit better.

I love to give to others, although half of the time I don't even realize I'm doing it. It's just something that comes naturally. A close friend of mine once told me I let people take advantage of my good nature. She thinks it's unfortunate that I do things for others but they don't always reciprocate. I, however, do not see it that way. Why do we have to get paid back for good deeds? If you're looking for a reward or something in return, then your kindness isn't sincere. There's nothing altruistic about expecting to be paid back. I enjoy giving of myself, and if I don't feel taken advantage of, then my friends shouldn't worry. I feel satisfied and fulfilled, and it's a beautiful thing. I have never, ever in my lifetime felt that I deserved repayment for any deed I have done for others. Now I look at how many wonderful people and how much love has come into my life, and I know that in a way,

I have been rewarded. It's a pleasant but unexpected side effect of being good to others.

We all have the ability to donate something to better each other's lives, whether it's through extending yourself to someone else in their time of need or just creating a lasting impression or memory that they can cherish. Instead of always looking inward and trying to figure out how to better our own lives, we should look around us and see the opportunities we have to help others. It is in giving that we receive. It is in sharing joy that we are fulfilled. It is in respecting each other that we receive respect. If everyone only realized the betterment of their own lives really depends on bettering the lives of others, the domino effect would be endless!

If you look at some of the happiest people you know, or at those people you admire who are living fulfilling lives, you'll notice they all have one thing in common. They all have taken the opportunity to give of themselves and make other people's lives happier. They're so content because they're experiencing the joy that comes with fulfilling their purpose in life. As I said earlier, we are here to help each other, and you'll find that when you do make the effort to help others, you are overcome with a feeling of bliss and contentment. That is the satisfaction of finding your purpose and seeing how you fit into the grand scheme of things. It's like being handed the answers to the mysteries of the universe, yet it's so simple to achieve. When you help others, you'll feel it. Suddenly, things will make sense, and you'll wonder why you hadn't been doing it all along!

One of my friends said to me the other day, "You are so selfless. You give of yourself regardless of what you receive in return. You are the nicest person I've ever known." Wow! That was a tremendous thing to hear. I was shocked to hear someone talk about me in such a way; I thought for sure she must have meant someone else, because I certainly don't view myself like that. I simply live my life the best way I know how.

I wanted to explain that the reason I am so fulfilled in every aspect of my life is because I give of myself each and every day. I almost wanted to say, "Try it, you can feel this way, too. It's so easy!" I think it's something that everyone knows deep down, but sometimes life and our own concerns get in the way. I want to believe that everyone has good in them, it's just that we have so much going on in our day to day lives, that it's easy to forget to take a minute out of your day to be charitable. Once you start making it part of your regular routine, though, it will become second nature. When I give of myself, I do it because I feel it's right and for no reason other than that. I never expect anything in return. Nothing. However, some people are not like that and it took me nearly half my life to realize that every time I do a good deed, many people wonder what my motive is. Before I've even finished what I'm doing, people are questioning why I'm doing it. I must drive people crazy, because I don't have any motives other than the fact that it just feels like a good thing to do. It's that simple.

I often like to think about the times when people have given selflessly to me and my family. When I think about how kind people have been to us, and how fortunate we are to experience the goodwill of others, it makes me want to do more to help those who need it. Giving is contagious. When you do a good deed for someone, you encourage them to do something for others.

We had just moved into a brand new neighborhood when I was diagnosed with kidney cancer. I didn't know anyone and hadn't even met all my neighbors yet. When I came home from the hospital, obviously I wasn't quite feeling up to doing all the work I normally would do to run the house. My mother moved in to help out while I recovered, but it wasn't easy for her. Between taking care of me and the children, my mother was exhausted, both physically and mentally. Watching her daughter recover from major surgery was definitely draining, let alone having to take care of my boys who were only five and seven years old at the time.

One of my neighbors coordinated with her woman's club, and they created a hot dinner circuit. Every single night, for weeks, there was a hot dinner for my family. At dinner time each night, people I didn't even know came to my house with hot home cooked meals for my family. Even after I had recovered, the kindness continued. I would meet people in town months later and they would ask me how I was feeling and say they were glad to see me up and around. I thanked them so much for everything they did and let them know how much my family appreciated the incredible support from the community. Our neighbors didn't even know us and yet each and every family was happy to help out in any way they could until I was back on my feet again, which took months. It was so touching to know how wonderfully giving people can be. It really is in the giving that we receive.

It's all about changing your attitude towards the world around you. Never say "What have you done for me lately?" but rather "What can I do for you?" Never say, "What's in it for me?" but feel, with sincerity, that it's nice to see someone else's happiness. Never let anyone else's sadness bring you down; instead do what you can to help them to achieve happiness. Never fear the future, but enjoy today and do your best to make the next day better. And most importantly, never say never!

Sometimes we get mad at people, even those we love, and we say terrible, hurtful things out of anger. It's very easy for silly arguments to quickly get out of control, and before you know it, it's a big misunderstanding. It's alright to be angry with someone if they do something hurtful toward you; that is human nature. But never say never! Don't say things like, "I'll never talk to you again," or, "I'll never forgive you." When you say things like that, what you're really saying is, "I'm going to hold on to this anger forever." Why would you want to do something like that? It's not going to make you feel better. It doesn't help anyone.

I believe in forgiveness. It's normal and healthy to get angry when you're hurt, but it is also healthy to forgive. When we forgive someone, we're releasing ourselves from the anger. I don't see forgiveness being about the other person. It's not about releasing them. It's about dropping that anger and resentment from your life, sweeping it under the table, and starting over. It's an act of kindness toward yourself. When we forgive someone, we free ourselves; forgiveness is freedom from the anger, guilt, and sadness we've been carrying around.

For many, many years, my mother did not speak with her sisters, Patty and Donna. It wasn't her choice. My mom actually attempted several times to keep in touch; however, letters she had written were returned and phone calls were never answered. For years she continued to send her sisters cards on the holidays and on their birthdays, but she never heard back from them. She wished that she could reunite with Patty and Donna, but she just couldn't get through to them.

Mom felt that the rift was started out of mounting years of jealousy. She explained that she never had any animosity toward them but that they had bad feelings toward her. Her sisters lived together and had never been married or had children. "They were jealous. I had children, I was married, and they also felt I was Mom's favorite," my mother told me. They felt that their parents had allowed my mother to finish her education, while they weren't able to do so, and had to move into the workplace. Mom had finished college and went on to finish up two masters degrees and began her career as a teacher. So Donna, the oldest sister, convinced Patty to break off contact with my mother, and that's the way things were until recently when Donna passed away.

After Donna passed, Patty was put in a nursing home by her lawyer who had power of attorney. It turned out that all my aunts' money was taken by their lawyer who relocated to Hawaii without leaving my aunts a penny. They had scrimped and saved all their lives to ensure they would be able to live comfortably after they retired, and now it was all gone. Mom finally found her only living sister in this nursing home, after much searching. My Aunt Patty suffers from dementia, yet recognized my mom and forgot all about their differences. They've resumed their friendship and now my mom visits her on a regular basis.

All these years have gone by but as mom says, "It feels like no time has passed." They picked up where they left off. My aunt was so happy to see all her nieces and nephews for the first time in years and we were happy to see her. Patty is seventeen years older than my mother, making her eighty-seven years old now. We were all so fortunate that Mom was able to locate her long lost sister before it was too late. Life is too short not to forgive and move on. The past should be left in the past.

Thank goodness for Mom's ability to forgive and move on otherwise she might have never had the opportunity to see her sister again. As it is, Mom is quite sad that she was unable to resume her relationship with her oldest sister who recently passed away. Now, at least, mom has this time to catch up with Patty. We can't let pride or our hurt feelings prevent us from forgiving. Being able to forgive her sisters became a blessing for my mother, and our whole family.

We must not only be forgiving of others, but of ourselves. We're only human. We are all allowed to be mad sometimes. We're allowed to be irritated or frustrated or foolish. These are all normal emotions, and there's nothing wrong with feeling that way sometimes. We all make mistakes, what's important is recognizing them and learning from them. Holding on to the negative feelings doesn't do anyone any good. Life is a journey, and we're not given a map. Sometimes we take a wrong turn and hit some rocky roads. That's just part of the ride. We all need to forgive ourselves for choices we make along the way.

I don't believe in regrets. Everything happens for a reason, and we can learn from every experience we face in life, even the unpleasant ones. As long as you continue to learn and grow, and push forward with an optimistic outlook, you should never look back on your past with regret. Every choice you make in life is part of a chain of events that leads you toward your next steps. They way you react to each situation effects what will happen next and how your life will turn out. Don't regret things that have happened in the past, they were stepping stones to the next phase of your life. Everything that happens in our lives has a purpose, and we may not see that purpose until our journey has reached its end, but we must trust that those unpleasant events in our lives were necessary to further our adventure.

I try to carry these positive philosophies through my life, and keep these things in mind when I encounter obstacles. When I meet new people, I always try and look for the good in them, and keep myself open to the possibilities of a new friendship. I don't believe in approaching situations with a skeptical outlook. Usually, if someone is unpleasant, I try to give them the benefit of the doubt and think about what reasons they might have for being that way. Everyone has a bad day sometimes! But just because you can understand someone's actions, there is no reason to put up with anyone who is not respectful. I steer clear of abusive people, those types who are intentionally mean to others. I have zero tolerance for people who are not respectful of other human beings. Everyone deserves to breathe the air equally and no one is better than the next, it doesn't matter who they are. It's the golden rule, "Do unto others as you would have others do unto you." Treat people how you would like them to treat you, it's very simple!

I attended a social function a while ago, and the room was filled with people discussing themselves. All they could talk about is what they owned, and what they had bought; everything was about material possessions. The amazing thing is these people were defining themselves by what they owned. They weren't talking about their beliefs, or their hobbies, or their families. Everything was about material goods. The conversations were as superficial as they could be.

I found it quite interesting, so I engaged in conversation with these people I had never met before. I found the whole evening fascinating, it certainly wasn't anything like how I live my life. My husband sized it up pretty well. He said the party was filled with a bunch of "wanna bes." They want to be more than they are, so they flaunt their money and their possessions to appear more important. They're not happy with themselves unless they have something to brag about. I think those who constantly talk about their material possessions appear to be somewhat insecure. Those who take the time to make it known that they drive an expensive sports car think it somehow places them further up the social ladder. In their minds, having expensive items makes them a more valuable person. What they really don't understand is that it makes them sound extremely superficial. What people need to realize is that we are all equal. No one is better or worse than anyone else in this life. Having expensive jewelry certainly isn't going to make you a better person!

I personally grew up around wealth and I never had the point of view that just because someone was wealthy, it made them better than those who were not as fortunate financially. One night, my husband and I went to dinner with another couple to a very exclusive restaurant. The woman I was sitting with was extremely rude to the wait staff. Her attitude was, "I'm paying good money for my meal, I deserve better service." Now, it is understandable that if you're paying a lot of money for a meal, you might be upset if your food doesn't come out quite right. That's no excuse to be nasty to people, though. Clearly, she felt that since she was paying so much for food, she had the right to treat the staff however she wanted. She blamed them for any trouble with her meal, and was pretty rude about it. It wasn't even the wait staff's fault that the chef had undercooked her dinner. The waiter graciously took it back and returned with the entrée cooked to her liking. Here was a wealthy woman who disregarded the feelings of the waiter for her own gratification. Her money didn't entitle her to be disrespectful to people. Yes, she's paying good money for her meal, but the waiters aren't being paid to take abuse from patrons, and they should never have to deal with that type of behavior. Needless to say, I was quite embarrassed for the woman and I could not wait for dinner to be over.

One should always be respectful, no matter what their occupation or social status. I am very grateful. I'm grateful for the busboy, the waiter, the chef, and the restaurant owner because these are the people who make my dining experience a pleasant one. They all do their part to make sure I enjoy my meal. Each and every one of these people deserves equal respect from their patrons, regardless of their patrons' wealth!

***

You know how the old expression goes . . . money isn't everything. It really isn't! I would define "everything" as health, happiness and love. These are the things that really matter in life. Material possessions are nice to have, but they'll never take the place of a close friend or a cherished family member. Money can't make you happy if you're not already fulfilled emotionally. Happiness comes from within; it is not something we can purchase. It comes from feeling loved and from feeling useful and from having faith that things will work out in the end. Happiness is about appreciating everything around you, and accepting yourself as you are.

It's so important to be happy with who you are, and to always stay true to yourself. It's an easy thing to say, but hard to define. I think being true to yourself means following your moral compass at all times. People will constantly try to tell you what they think is right, and what they think is wrong. Their ideas may not always be what is right for you. You have to look inside yourself and see which way that compass is pointing. If you listen to your heart, you'll always know what to do. You must never forfeit yourself to do what someone else thinks is right. If it doesn't feel right to you, you have to listen to your instincts.

Years ago, I was employed by one of the most reputable publishing companies in the world, doing market research work. My job was to work with numbers and statistics, to figure out what advertising strategies would work best for our clients. I was brought into a meeting with one of the VPs who wanted to understand more about the results of a market research study I had conducted on behalf of one of our clients. I explained that the results of the study were not stable because the sample base was too small. The sampling error was too high to project the data. If the sample base was high enough, the data was extremely favorable. In other words, we hadn't talked to enough people to make an accurate prediction, but based on the small group we had interviewed, the numbers looked good. Of course, with this type of research, you need a very large sampling group. Just because the results looked favorable with a small group, it doesn't mean that the statistics will be the same when more people are interviewed. Sometimes the data can shift completely when you get a larger sampling.

Well, the VP asked, if we went ahead and doubled the base, would the numbers be stable. I said back to him, "You can't do that." I knew that wasn't the right way to conduct research, you can't just double the numbers without actually having a larger base.

The VP looked at me and said, "I'm not asking you, I'm telling you." Well, I couldn't do it. Now here I was, a research manager, telling one of the major

VPs at this well respected corporation that I would not do what he asked. Without another thought, I started looking for a new job and within weeks I left the company.

Not only in business, but in life, ethics are everything. We need to stand up for what we believe in and always do the right thing no matter what the cost. It wasn't easy for me to give up my job, but I knew I couldn't continue to work there. Even if I wanted to, I probably wouldn't have been welcome after defying such a high-ranking VP. I wasn't willing to cheat on the statistics in order to keep my job. I knew denying his request would result in my having to leave the job, but I wasn't going to sacrifice my morals just to stay employed. I ended up landing a job on Long Island that paid more money and the commute was much shorter than the commute I had previously been making to Manhattan. It had been very scary to leave my job, but I ended up in a much better situation. It felt as if I was being rewarded for being honest. Life may seem scary or bleak at times, but in the end, everything seems to fall into place. As long as you're true to yourself and follow your heart, you will always find your way through dark times.

***

With each passing generation, we evolve technologically, spiritually and intellectually. Technologically we are evolving in a positive direction, and the same goes for our spiritual and intellectual evolution. Everything is moving forward. However, it seems that with every passing generation, our moral values are becoming less and less important. Years ago, it was unheard of to be intimately involved prior to marriage. Now, not only are most people engaging in sexual activity before they are married, but many of those who are sexually active are young teenagers. Crime rates have risen, divorce rates are out of control, where has all the decency gone? Morally, it appears that our society is heading toward destruction.

Though we are moving in a forward direction technologically, spiritually and intellectually, our evolution as a species is hindered by our lack of morality. The morality component is so important to the existence of future generations; it is the very basis of a structured and civilized society. With each passing day, the news brings us stories of unthinkable violence and corruption. How do we stop the immorality, the wickedness, and the fact that people are losing genuine respect for each other as human beings? How are we to keep our moral state of health in check for generations to come? We must make a difference in our own lives and hope we set examples for others to follow. It has to start at home and in the schools. Parents and teachers cannot demand respect, they must earn it from their children, and the only way children learn respect is through the example of their parents and teachers. Children live what they learn. It is up to us to live ethical, honest lives, and make principled decisions to set an example for the future generation.

If the world were just a kinder place, life would be so much better. Instead of being quick to judge or quick to assume, we should be quick to help and quick to strive to understand other people's points of view. Most misunderstandings among people come from the lack of understanding about each other's situations and perspectives. We, as a society, have to become more empathetic in order to better understand other people's points of view. Parents need to teach their children empathy, it is a learned behavior. To show a child the result of an action, whether it is a verbal or physical action, is extremely important in teaching a child to make better choices. It's also very important to understand where a person is coming from. Too often, the person listening imposes their own perspective on what they're hearing, and they never really see it from the speaker's point of view. When you look at people's intentions from a defensive standpoint, then there's no hope for understanding. However, if you look at people's intentions from where they truly stem, it makes all the sense in the world, and there's nothing to get defensive about. It is all a matter of communication, and realizing that not everyone is thinking the same way you are.

It's important to remember that everyone is unique. What is good for us is not always what is good for others, and vice versa. Only you can know what is best for you, and you must keep in mind that this is true for all people. Everyone likes to give their opinion and offer advice to their friends, but we often forget to think about the other person's point of view. It's very easy to be disappointed by someone else's advice or recommendations. Your friends may tell you, "You have to try this great restaurant," or, "I know a great place to shop for home furnishings." Now, it may be great to the person who is recommending these places, but everyone is so different and we all have our own unique tastes and preferences. Those who recommend things really have to know a lot about the person they're recommending to if they want their suggestions to be useful, and vice versa. How do you recommend a great Chinese restaurant to someone who doesn't like Chinese food?!

The other day, I took a dear friend for a quick bite to eat at a Chinese bistro in the shopping mall. My sister-in-law has taken me there and we both think it's terrific! I just assumed my friend would think so, too. Well, she didn't like it one bit! I should not have assumed she even liked Chinese food! I didn't even think about it. I just assumed that everyone likes Chinese food, but I didn't take into account that my friend is Armenian. She grew up in a different culture, with different types of foods, and completely different taste. I'm using the example of Chinese food, but the real point is, you shouldn't make assumptions about other people and what they like. We are all very different, and it's important to get to know a person and take their personal preferences into consideration. Fortunately, my friend wasn't too upset about the Chinese food, but a situation like this could have been very insulting or embarrassing. What if there was something in the food that violated my friend's religion or personal beliefs? I should have asked her if she liked Chinese food before taking her, and considered her culture and background before making assumptions.

It's very easy to assume everyone else thinks the way we do, and likes what we like. After all, our experiences are all we know, and it can be difficult to imagine what other peoples lives are like. People love to give advice, but it's often advice that only works for them. It's really hard to offer advice without the advice being biased toward our own experiences. That's why I always say you have to look within yourself to find the answers.

Trust your instincts and follow your moral compass. You're the only one that can decide what is right for you. When other people give you advice, be appreciative of the kind gesture they are making, but keep in mind that they are speaking from their own experience, and probably can't relate to your situation. As you go through your life, learn from everything that happens to you. Pay attention to the events that transpire, and you'll figure out what works for you and what doesn't. You have a lifetime of experiences to learn from, so trust yourself to make the right decisions. Always listen to your heart.

9

Living:
If you're not living in the positive zone, you're not living.

I AM NOW going to share with you a series of events that led up to what I believe to be an incredible miracle. Recently, I was with a friend of mine at a car wash that I've been going to since I first got my driver's license. We were waiting for our cars and I looked up at the sign, realizing that I had never noticed before that the name of this place I had been visiting all these years was "Miracle Car Wash." I thought it was strange that I had been there so many times and never noticed the name, but other than that, I didn't think much of it. A few moments went by and I went to put on my lip gloss that I've been wearing for awhile. I happened to look at the name of this lip gloss after I applied it, and the name of it was "Miracle." I looked at my friend, who also wore the same lip gloss, and asked her if she ever noticed that her lip gloss was called "Miracle." She had never noticed it, either. "Well that's two miracles," I said, "All I need is one more."

Well, you're not going to believe this, my surgeon called me first thing the next morning and told me that the tumor they found located on the wall outside the right kidney was not there. The scan I had during my regular check-up showed a tumor about the size of a pea outside my right kidney. It was the same kidney I had previously had a tumor on, and it looked like they were going to have to operate again. Five weeks later, I had a renal protocol CT scan for a more definitive look at the tumor and its exact location, and it was not there. I asked the surgeon where it had gone and the surgeon said, "It's just not there."

I said, "What do you mean it's just not there?" It didn't make any sense!

She said, repeatedly, "It's just not there!" No one had any idea what happened or why it disappeared, but it was great news for me! No surgery, no recovery, and best but certainly not least, I get to keep my kidney! Or should I say, what's left of it from the first surgery over a year and a half earlier, when they removed a malignant tumor. It just doesn't get better than that! What a miracle!

Things are happening all around us that sometimes we just can't see. It's all so incredible! I was told that I had another tumor that would have to be removed, but a few weeks later, the tumor disappeared from the CT scan screen! O.K., so where did it go? I truly believe it is a testament of my faith! My faith brought me through everything in my life thus far, and it has even brought me to what appears to be a miracle. Despite my cancer diagnosis, I have made it a point to live an optimistic, positive life. I believed things would work out for the best, and that I could get through my illness. I wasn't going to let it defeat me, and it hasn't. Everything always works out, you just have to believe.

It's been a few years since I was diagnosed with kidney cancer and every time I think or say the word cancer, it is still unreal to me. To most people, the word "cancer" means sickness and death. But I'm not sick and I'm not dying, I'm very much alive and kicking! Sure, I have some rough days, but I'm not going to go through life being a "sick" person. As long as I can still enjoy my days, I will. Of course, that doesn't mean I don't think about the illness. Though I know in my heart I am almost 100% "cured", I am constantly aware of the fact that one day it might return. But that knowledge doesn't stop me, I don't let "what ifs" keep me down. I won't let fear paralyze me. My illness invigorates me, it drives me to live.

I cherish every moment, because I know that I could leave this earth at any time. Remember, the moment is all you have. Find the beauty in it. Run barefoot on the beach, drive a convertible with the top down, sing as loud as you can to the song on the radio, tell someone who you love that you love them. Don't let the day pass without doing something to make that day worthwhile. It is so easy to get caught up in the humdrum of life. Don't forget to take a moment to simply enjoy living. Sometimes one beautiful hour in a day offsets the rest of the twenty-three hours that weren't so wonderful. Learn to find these moments and hold on to them.

Life is a series of brief moments and experiences. Through them all, we are constantly learning. We are born. We learn to cry. We learn to walk. We learn to speak. We learn to understand. We learn to accept. We learn to face our fears. We learn to overcome our anxieties. We learn to make the best of any situation. We learn to accept things for what they are. We learn to enjoy life. We learn to cope. We learn about pain and suffering. We learn to adapt. We learn what human nature is all about. We learn how to be a better person. We learn to love, over and over again. It is a constant series of events, and through it all, we grow.

Every moment of our lives takes us to the next. Even those unpleasant moments of our lives are valuable, because they teach us important lessons and effect how we approach the rest of our lives. Everything falls into place the way it's meant to. It may not make sense at the time; you may wonder, "Why is this happening to me?" but eventually you will see how that moment led you down a path that brought you to where you are now. It couldn't have happened any other way, everything in your life happened for a reason, to bring you to the point you are at now. Every moment is important.

You know the old expression, "You take the good with the bad." Well, there's no other way to take life, because it definitely has its share of both. We just have to make it through the tough times and make sure we appreciate and enjoy the good times, as well. Don't let the bad parts of life overwhelm you. You must realize that there is always a balance. There will always be good, and there will always be bad, so look for the good.

So many people expect life to be full of good times, constant fun and excitement. People who live like this do not enjoy the moment, the simple pleasures that life brings to them. They're always looking for more, for something better, rather than seeing how wonderful things are already. Like I always say, I'm just grateful everyday when I open my eyes and I am thankful for each day in which I am able to be an active participant. Life is full of simple pleasures.

It's better to appreciate what you have then to strive for more. That isn't to say that you shouldn't reach for your dreams and try and make your life better. What I mean is, don't look at your life and think things aren't good enough. Realize how wonderful life is now, and be grateful for what you have. When you constantly desire more, you will never be happy. If you're always looking for something new, something better, you can never be satisfied. Be happy with what you have. Did you ever notice that when we strive for something and it comes to us, either through hard work or just by chance, after a while the novelty of that particular thing we desired wears off. The feeling only lasts for a little while and then we're back to square one, wanting something newer and better. We should appreciate things the way they are and not strive for those things we think will make us happier. If you constantly desire something, and you're never able to obtain it, you will spend your life yearning for the unreachable, instead of simply enjoying your life. After I found out I had cancer, I realized that the greatest treasures in life are already all around me. I have my family and my friends, I have my life, and I'm going to enjoy it exactly the way it is. I don't need material things or expensive gadgets; I've learned what is truly important. If you learn to appreciate what you have, you will always be happy.

It's love, family and friendships that keep us happy. Those are the things we should be thankful for every day. Who else could we share our happiness with if it wasn't for our family and friends? The things that make us happy, money can't buy. Take, for instance, when you finally buy your dream car. It's quite a thrill at first, but over time, that dream car becomes just a means of transportation. The thrill won't last for long. What about your dream house? You can spend all your money on the biggest, fanciest house you find. After a while, your dream house simply becomes a home. It can only be as warm and wonderful as the people in it. That love would have existed in any house, regardless of the price. It's not about the look or the design, it is about the love that inhabits the home. The price tag isn't what makes people happy.

***

I was speaking to a friend of mine quite a while ago and we were talking about her dad. She said he was a changed man since he was diagnosed with colon cancer. She said he really started enjoying life much more. I think about that and I can honestly say that I truly couldn't enjoy life any more than I already do. I understand what she meant, though. Facing something like cancer makes you realize how precious life is. Being diagnosed with cancer is like having someone tell you, "You can die at any time." Of course, that's true for everyone; death is a part of life and none of us know when we might leave this earth. However, we don't usually think about that. When you get a disease like cancer, it forces you to think about it. You realize that you must cherish every moment you have in life, because you may not have the opportunity for long. It's not a pessimistic view; it's a very optimistic one. It helps you see how beautiful and valuable life is, and how incredible it is to be alive. I really think that those of us who have been diagnosed with potentially fatal diseases learn to enjoy life more than the average person. I only hope that through this book, I can help everyone to see life the way I do. I want to teach people to be grateful for every breath they take, and thankful for all the small wonders around them. Life is a gift and we must all treat it that way.

My friend Diane is an incredible inspiration to me, and to everyone who knows her. She is someone who really appreciates how precious life is. Diane had three children and was contemplating a fourth. She wasn't sure if she was ready for another, but with a little push from her friends, she decided to go for it. To Diane, family was everything. So the idea of having another child to love and care for was wonderful to her. At the same time, she was always giving of herself to help others. She always made a hot prepared meal for families that were in need, whether it was a sick friend or a family whose mom was in the hospital having another baby. Diane always seemed to have her priorities in place. So she became pregnant again, and amazingly, she found herself with two little blessings instead of one. Twins! Diane's pregnancy was going fine, I guess as fine as it could be carrying twins at nearly forty years old. After giving birth, Diane and the new babies appeared to be alright, so her husband left the hospital to tend to the three little ones at home.

Shortly after sharing the news with their family, Diane's husband Ted returned to the hospital. As he was walking across the parking lot, he saw his brother-in-law screaming for him. "Come quick," he screamed, "Hurry up! It's your wife! They need your consent to operate!" Ted ran as fast as he could into the hospital to sign the papers, and off Diane went into the operating room.

Apparently, right after Ted had left the hospital, his wife, Diane, experienced a severe headache that wouldn't go away. The pain was so unbearable that she called for the nurse. The nurse thought it was just a headache, and wanted to give her Tylenol but Diane knew something was very wrong. She said to the nurse, "You better get a doctor in here, I don't feel well," and then immediately passed out. Diane suffered a brain aneurism after giving birth to her twin boys.

Ted happened to be back just in time to sign the papers to admit her into the operating room, and thank god that nurse happened to be by Diane's side when she lost consciousness. If not for this impeccable timing, Diane wouldn't be here to enjoy every single one of her five wonderful children. As I always say, timing is everything! Well, needless to say, the road ahead for Diane and her family was quite rocky. She had to relearn how to walk and how to talk. She even had to relearn how to do routine duties like brush her teeth, and wash her face. Everything was a struggle.

Diane's recovery is truly a miracle. I am so thankful that there are wonderful doctors out there who truly have the gift of healing, and that Diane happened to be in the right place at the right time to receive their help.

Diane never gave up. She worked long and hard to gain back all of her motor functions. As a result of this tragedy, Diane began to help others with brain trauma and used her struggle to make a difference in many people's lives. Diane could have chosen to feel sorry for herself and become introverted, but instead, she became a motivational speaker for those who needed her help. She is an inspiration to those who have experienced terrible tragedies. It can be very easy for someone who has undergone this kind of trauma to give up hope. It takes an incredible amount of work and dedication to regain motor skills and muscle function, but Diane shows people that it is possible. She lets them know that if they keep trying, they can achieve anything.

If Diane could overcome this setback, and emerge as a strong, healthy, amazing person, I know I can face anything that comes my way. Sometimes I have a very hard time dealing with my illness, but I try to remember that as long as you have hope, all things are possible. It can be difficult to keep that positive attitude, because cancer changes everything inside of you. You never know how you will feel from one day to the next, and things can go wrong very suddenly. Prior to my illness, nothing kept me down. I was always on the go; I always had something to do and somewhere to be. When I got sick, things changed.

I would be lying in bed not feeling well, and I'd think to myself, "Who is this person lying here?" I barely recognized myself, and it was a very scary feeling. I knew that I couldn't change the circumstances of my illness, but I could still do my best to enjoy life and make the most of my time. I find that keeping busy helps me get through the tough times. Having distractions keeps your mind off the negative thoughts. And what better way to keep busy than to continue to go through your daily routine! Taking care of the kids, working, chores, they all help, so keep on living life like you normally do!

I have to look at my friends like Diane, who have gotten past terrible illness, and tell myself that there is hope. My life was completely turned around when I became sick, and I'd be lying if I told you it wasn't a struggle. However, we all have the ability to turn a struggle into an opportunity to live a better life. We just have to view these events as reminders to appreciate what we have. Do not put off appreciating your life, you have to love it the exact way it is. Could it be better? I'm sure it could. Could it be worse? Absolutely! We have no real control over which direction our life will lead us; however, we can surely figure out a way to enjoy the ride. Life is filled with tragedies, mishaps, disappointments, and time and time again it falls short of our expectations. But life is also filled with so many wonderful opportunities to seize; there are hundreds of them every day. All we need to do is look around and pick one.

My husband's love is something that I truly appreciate and that keeps my mind off my illness. Every day he tells me how he wouldn't be whole without me, that I complete him and that I have no idea just how much he loves me. But I do know. I know he loves me more than anything, and in a way, my illness has only strengthened that. We now realize that our time together might be limited, and every moment is precious so we have to make the most of it. We express our love every day, as much as possible, and I know that I wouldn't be as positive as I am if it weren't for Fred's love. He gives me something to live for, something to fight for.

Having a special partner in life not only lessens the burdens we face, but the joys of life are that much more pleasurable when you have someone to share it with. Having friends who accept you for who you are makes it easier to deal with difficulties because you know there's someone who cares. Having children to tell you they love you at the end of a bad day dissolves all that misery and puts life into perspective. We are constantly surrounded by those things that put life into perspective, but all too often, we take those things for granted.

It's so important that we remember the positive things in our lives; the love, the friendship, all the small blessings. When we're dealing with death and hardship, these are the things that will pull us through the grief and help us to live again. Always remember that no matter what happens, your heart will endure. We have the incredible capability to deal with pain and suffering, and continue on. Everyone in the world deals with some form of tragedy, and yet they all keep on going, living their lives. You can, too.

I wrote a poem about positive thinking which reflects the way I view the world around me.

"Think Positive"

Positive thoughts and comments are all that we need
Not that of sorrow or struggle or horror, indeed
The world has enough of that to more than last
So try to think positive, you just might have a blast
Life is filled with so much, even we can't comprehend
The kind of stuff that is unbearable to discuss with family
or friends
More positive thoughts and comments need to come from
within
So that the world at least appears a better place to live in
It is within our own minds, our outlook effects who we'll
be
So have more positive thoughts, you'll be happier, you'll
see
Does it happen overnight? Absolutely, positively not
But you must start right now. Think positive, give it your
best shot
For today is all we have and that's a good thing to
understand
We must seize the day. Have fun or lend a hand
Share with others. Be genuine. Just reach out to those in
need
It helps make your world more positive, happiness comes
with each good deed
Let more positive thoughts take over your own thinking
Before you know it, you'll be smiling, laughing and
winking!
If the whole world had a choice, it would be happy, that's its
desire
So start with you. Its contagious, it will spread like wild
fire
Life's what we make it to be
Positive thoughts are truly the key

It's not in mulling over what you did wrong yesterday or what happened in the past
It's charging forward to see what tomorrow brings, because life goes way too fast
There's no time to stop and contemplate your life, nor what possibly will come
For it is this moment you must enjoy, and gather strength from
So in closing, there are just a few more things I'd like to share

Enjoy your days, think positive, don't get caught up in life's despair
So when life feels somewhat dull and you're down or feeling blue
Don't forget that happiness lies only within you
Make the best of the moment for tomorrow may or may not be
Go to the beach, call a friend, or simply say "I'm happy to be me."
Eventually, you will awaken each day, ready to conquer what's ahead
You will actually look forward to getting out of bed

For whatever the day brings you there's just one thing to remember
Your approach to life should be positive whether it's August or December!

***

Always remember that the true meaning of life, simply put, is that we are here to make the world a better place. Period. It's not about us, it's all about others! Carry that message through all of your days.

The more you give of yourself to others, the more fulfilled your life will be, it is as easy as that. Remember, life is just a blip of time here on earth. The older we get, the faster it goes! So, make it count!

When we truly give of ourselves, in whatever capacity we are doing it, we must not, even for a moment, think, "Well, where is this going to get me? If I do this, this, and that, then maybe I will get something in return." If you approach a good deed looking for a reward or recognition, you will set yourself up for disappointment over and over and over again. You will not become famous or rich from doing good deeds! The point of giving is not to get something in return; it is simply to do good.

With society the way it is, though, every one thinks good deeds come with an ulterior motive. That's why I hear over and over again from my own friends, "Oh, I owe you one."

My answer again and again is, "No, you don't owe me anything! Whatever it is that I did, I did it because I wanted to do it. I didn't do it expecting to receive anything in return." Now, think about those people who say the words, "I owe you one." Those people are obviously counting whose turn it is, aren't they? Don't waste your life keeping score. Spend your time doing more meaningful things!

Take the time to let people know how you feel. It is so important to let people know how much they mean to you because you never know if you will have that opportunity again. And even if they already know, it still feels good to hear it! Don't let another day go by without telling your loved ones what they mean to you. If you're holding any grudges, or are angry over something that happened between you in the past, let it go! Forgiving will free you from the negative feelings, and you'll be so much happier. Think about it, if you left this earth tomorrow, would you want to leave it on those terms, with that anger lingering? Think about what's really important in the grand scheme of things. If you lived to be one hundred years old, do you think that you'll still be worrying about the petty arguments you had with your friends and family? Or will you be wishing that you had seen past your anger and spent more quality time with them? No one wants to die with regrets, so live your life like every day is your last! It's not morbid, it's life affirming. It makes you see what's truly important.

Don't let life consume you. Consume life! There are times in our lives where we just get caught up in letting the little things rule us instead of remembering that our time here is so short. We should spend more time doing the things we enjoy instead of worrying about what we're supposed to be doing. We can satisfy our daily responsibilities of work and chores and taking care of the kids, while still seizing the moment and enjoying life. Just because you have to go shop for groceries doesn't mean you can't marvel at the beautiful day outside and linger in the sunshine. Life doesn't have to be a chore! It's all a matter of perspective. If your perception is that your daily routine is a hassle, then it will be. But if you look at it as an opportunity to enjoy the wonders around you, life will be so much more pleasant!

My days could obviously be numbered and like I've done in the past, I'm going to live each and every day like it is my last. I will enjoy each and every moment I spend with my family and friends as if everything is going to be O.K. And you know what? It will be! Though I am still human and am still very saddened by this turn of events, I can see the silver lining. Even if I'm not here much longer, I know I've been blessed with a wonderful life, and I'm going to appreciate every moment that I have left. I am going to make sure that I take pleasure in each day that I have here on Earth. I will spend time with my husband and my children, and know that every minute with them is a blessing. I want them to have fond, loving memories of me if I am gone, and so I'm not going to spend my days depressed and complaining. I am going to be cheerful and effervescent, just as I've always been. I don't want my loved ones to remember me as a sickly person, I want them to think of me the way I've been all my life. I will continue to be joyous and positive, because there is no other way to be. When you're pessimistic and miserable, that simply isn't living. I know that my life is precious, and I will enjoy it to the end, and that is truly a blessing!

Acknowledgements

First and foremost… I thank God

Special thanks to the following people…

Joanne Starrer
Editor and friend… who is truly talented in her ability to bring my voice to print

Linda Langton
Literary Agent… who spent much time and effort trying to publish "Blessed Beyond Words"

Norayr Demirciyan
Composer of my first song "Your Guardian Angel"

Diana Liotta
Mom… who always believed in me and couldn't wait to share this book with all our family and friends!

Dr. Casmiro Liotta
Dad… who helped to shape the person I am today

Eric Liotta , Casey Liotta, Amy Liotta, Eve-lynn Liotta Blonder, John Liotta
All my siblings who will always be near and dear to my heart

Printed in the United States
50132LVS00001B/148-513

9 781425 931278